HELPING CHILDREN COPE WITH DIVORCE

ROSEMARY WELLS grew up in Scotland and England, and settled in Africa when she married. Returning to England, she was widowed and left with young children. She is a former teacher, and still enjoys teaching writers' workshops, but she is now a professional writer. Her first book, *Helping Children Cope with Grief*, has become essential reading for all those helping a child through a bereavement. She is also the author of *Your Grandchild and You*.

Overcoming Common Problems

HELPING CHILDREN COPE WITH DIVORCE

Rosemary Wells

sheldon PRESS

First published in Great Britain in 1989 by
Sheldon Press, SPCK, Marylebone Road, London NW1 4DU

Revised and updated editions 1993, 1997

British Library Cataloguing in Publication Data

A catalogue record for this book is available from the British Library

ISBN 0–85969–777–0

Photoset by Deltatype Ltd, Birkenhead, Merseyside
Printed in Great Britain by
Biddles Ltd, Guildford and King's Lynn

Contents

Acknowledgements

I would like to thank the following people for their professional advice, expert help, generous time and enthusiastic interest during the research and writing of this book:

Elizabeth Andrews, Peter Ball, Gill Cashdom, Debbie Derrick, Thelma Fisher, Kate Gardiner, Fred Gibbons, Patricia Harris, Shirley Hefferman, Judy Hildebrand, Sonya Hinton, Julia Nelki, Lisa Parkinson, Bruce Pearce, Jane Reardon, Richard Sax, Dee Slater.

I am gratefully indebted to those organizations who allowed me to study their work with divorced families, including: The National Stepfamily Association, The Tavistock Clinic, The National Council for One-Parent Families, The Children's Legal Centre, Families Need Fathers, 'Off Centre' at Hackney, The Saturday Centre in Balham, and several Gingerbread groups.

A very special thank you to all the families—children, parents and grandparents—who shared their experiences with me, and to the many pupils and teachers who willingly discussed the viewpoints within their schools. Also to the University research groups, psychiatrists, therapists and counsellors, church leaders, welfare and probation officers, all of whom so readily made available their books and papers. My sincere thanks to Diana Parker, who took time to read and edit the original legal content.

Finally, I owe a large debt of gratitude to Nigel Shepherd, Partner with solicitors Lace Mawer in Manchester and Chairman of SFLA 1995/1997, for giving so generously of his time and care to the professional checking of this revised edition.

Preface

Since this book was first published in 1989, the divorce rate in Britain has risen steadily and is now the highest in Europe. In England and Wales two out of five marriages end in divorce, meaning that one in 22 children will experience their parents' divorce by the age of five and one in four by the age of 16.

Because of these statistics, divorce is accepted today as a normal part of life. So the traumas, problems and emotional pain these children suffer are largely ignored, except by professionals in the law, in social work and psychiatry.

Legislation is constantly seeking to make divorce less complicated, but emotional divorce is no easier. There is often one parent who does not want the divorce. And almost without exception, children *never* want their parents to separate. That leaves a great many young people needing help. They have to come to terms with a situation over which they have no control.

Solicitors, probation and welfare officers, mediators and conciliators, therapists and counsellors, are growing more aware of the roles they must play—giving real help through listening and guiding, and by showing parents that it is up to *them* to make the decisions concerning their children. In the past, many such professionals either made all the decisions themselves or told the parents which ones to make. Parents often need help in communicating with each other *in their roles as parents*, no longer as husband and wife.

Family therapy enables children to have *their* say—ensuring that parents listen to their youngsters but do not burden them with impossible choices and decisions which would divide their loyalties even more severely.

There are few professions, agencies, groups or individuals who are not in positions where they could help children. Schools, the one place children *all* attend, are in an ideal position to assess if and when support is needed; 'Good parenting' might well be added to their extra curricular subjects. Churches, many of which stress the importance of premarital counselling, often include advice on parenting. Many understanding church leaders are now offering help to divorcing couples who wish to remain in their faith without the burden of 'guilt'. I hope they are offering similar support to the children.

Prenatal classes are now attended by both mothers and fathers. It would seem appropriate for the organizers to offer counselling in parenting—as well as the deep breathing and nappy changing! Warning young parents of the huge responsibility they are giving themselves might alert them to the seriousness of separating once they are mothers and fathers. If one or other is left to cope alone, through death or divorce, such training would be invaluable.

I have drawn on the expertise and experience of many professionals in legal, medical, psychiatric, educational and social welfare fields. I have spoken with parents and children in numerous situations before, during and after a divorce in the family. They have all shared their views, and they all, including the children, want to help young people who are facing similar problems—practical and emotional—through no fault of their own. For that reason, they were most generous in telling me their stories.

If any of their experiences can bring a fresh insight, or help any reader to 'know how it feels', then hopefully when they find themselves amongst a sadly divided family, they will feel better able to offer help to the confused children.

R.W.

1
Living in an Unhappy Home

Mother: My divorce has nothing to do with you.
Daughter (11): It has *everything* to do with me.

Children, when given a chance to state their views, want their parents to stay together. Many will go to *any* lengths to ensure that they do.

Even amongst the experts, there are widely differing opinions as to how great an effect the separation of parents may have on a child's development. Some argue that growing up within an *un*happy marriage is more damaging than the experience of separation. Others vehemently believe the opposite to be true. Both sides quote cases which confirm their findings, although many are contained within selective groups, such as psychiatric or child guidance clinics. It is an argument that can never be resolved accurately. Each family is unique.

Without doubt, within some families, the children may be hurt *less* by the divorce than by the marriage: for example, where one parent is violent or abusive, perhaps an alcoholic or drug addict. In other families, one parent (usually the father) is constantly away from home due to work, or totally disinterested in his children. In such cases, if the remaining parent can continue to give as much mental, emotional and social security to the children as they have always known, then the divorce may do them no more harm than the marriage.

But if the children's nurturing and needs are put in second place, or not even considered, then they may well be better off as they were—change in itself can be a cause of extreme stress.

Listening to the children

For me, the most significant survey, albeit small, carried out by Thames Television in London, came up with a finding none of us should ignore. Their survey resulted in a unanimous opinion—arrived at after *listening to children* talking. Their homes, in most cases, were far from happy in the accepted sense. Many were filled with bitter verbal or physical fighting, several children were victims of neglect. But, with only one exception, the children felt their lives would have been happier if their parents had *not* separated.

This fact alone should guide all adults/parents away from the old assumption that *they* know what is best for children. Many thoughtful, caring parents arrange their actions 'in the best interests of the family', genuinely believing they are fulfilling their parental duties with love and common sense.

Social workers, whose counselling skills should alert them to a child's needs, still tend to make their decisions on the grounds that 'We know what is best for the child'. Such decisions can cause havoc in a child's life, often with long-lasting effect. A district nurse recalls saying to a seven-year-old: 'You look a bit sad today, Pete,' and receiving the indignant reply: 'Of course I am, my mum and dad don't live together any more.'

Home sweet home

Children may rebel against discipline, and even before their teens begin to resent parental authority—but they do appreciate the stability of a home.

Sadly, there are those for whom divorce of their parents, who may or may not be married to each other, has little effect on them because their homes are so chaotic anyway. Paddy and Brian used to be punished for fighting, but night after night they would hear their parents having violent arguments, throwing things and 'behaving like kids themselves'.

It is easy to assess such homes as destructive for a child's emotional development. However, most youngsters become used to their own home: they *know* dad gets angry when drunk; they *know* mum is often out when they get home from school; they are *used to* their parents only talking through the children—that's their home. Only if dad threatens to leave, or mum talks of abandoning them, is real security at stake. That seems to be when the anxiety starts.

Sam, aged eight, said: 'My parents yelled at each other and mum would cry, and dad would drive off in his lorry. I was scared he would crash and leave mum and me alone.' Not a hint that they might separate; then when they did, he was shattered. 'Well, a home isn't a family without a mum and a dad, is it?'

It is not only the violent homes where children are confused. Kate and Andy's home was in a 'good' neighbourhood, with all the material things of life they needed. 'Perhaps we were naive for children in the 70s,' says Kate. 'Daddy was away so often we never thought it odd when mummy asked other men to the house; but when they separated it was like a sudden death.' For me, that is as sad as a family constantly fighting—it is not hate that is the opposite of love, but indifference.

Whatever the situation, few children will *not* suffer. The vital priority is for all involved in their care to ensure that this suffering is recognized and alleviated. So much depends on the relationships within a family. A decision taken for one family will seldom suit another.

Two teenage boys told me: 'If only dad had left years ago, we would all have relaxed. He never spoke to mum for years, and she often tried to overdose. Now she's a different person.'

Infidelity

A basic cause of divorce is often the unfaithfulness of one or other partner. For children, the realization that their parents are less than perfect is often overwhelmingly sad—with traumatic effects.

Jill was fifteen when her father had an affair with a girl of twenty. Her mother told Jill all the sordid details:

> My sister and I loved dad—the idea of him going with a young girl was horrid. We felt sort of let down by dad, yet upset at mum reading dad's letters and being so vindictive. By the time they separated we couldn't respect either of them.

Gwen was only eight when she found her mother in bed with a neighbour:

> I went to my room and cried for hours—I wasn't sure why. At supper mum never said a word, so I didn't either. But a few weeks later dad left us, and for years I hated mum as I thought it was all her fault. We never talked about it and she never remarried.

Not many marriages survive in these circumstances, and yet seldom are any explanations given to children. 'It's obvious, isn't it?' asked a young father whose wife had run off with his best friend. But for a child it needs careful discussion: she needs a chance to voice *her* thoughts, *her* fears—which may be even worse than the reality. Adults should never *assume* that a child has correctly summed up a situation. Their perceptions vary widely, depending upon age and intelligence.

Mother and father for life

Another issue on which some experts put forward opposing views is that of whether children benefit from continuing contact with both parents. Some argue that weekly visits, or holiday trips, with the non-custodial parent, are unsettling; they suggest a complete break to help the children 'forget' the parent they do not live with.

An important message from children cuts through these theories: they *all* desperately want a *continuing* relationship with both parents:

> If they don't let me see my dad I'd rather he was dead. Then I could visit his grave. He's my dad for ever and ever.

If stepparents come on the scene, the children still feel the same—perhaps even more strongly. No one can take the place of your mother or father (Chapter 7). Graham's was a real cry of despair when his father moved away: 'But he *must* live at home—he's my dad!'

There are unique, tragic cases where one parent abandons the family home in exceptional circumstances. But most experts now confirm that frequent, tension-free, contact with *both* parents not only minimizes a loss, but is 'profoundly helpful' to a child's adjustment to divorce.

Divorce as a major loss

The main difference between divorce and bereavement is that during a divorce period there is no specified 'time of loss' as there is with a death. The unhappy times prior to, during and following the divorce proceedings are very long indeed—so it is far more difficult to say when a child is beginning to 'accept' it. They are confused, sometimes not knowing *which* parent they will lose. Their world has shattered, yet all the people in it are still alive. For this reason, it can all become far more demanding and hard to handle—at the same time attracting far less sympathy than bereavement.

After either loss, there is the danger of a child fantasizing over the lost parent. A parent who has died may be idolized—built up into an unreal, saint-like figure. After divorce, the absent parent can be thought of as an ogre—a wicked person. Both fantasies should be discouraged—children need truth, happy memories and realistic contacts.

Clinging to a dream

The consequences are not obvious at first: on the one hand a child, because his parents *are* alive, will often feel there is a chance they may get together again. Even after a remarriage, children cling to their dream of life reverting to the original, complete family—all part of the 'denial' of what has happened. On the other hand, it does make acceptance more difficult—the final decree may be a turning point for the *parents*, but not for the *children*. *They* are not divorcing. They are having to grapple with the problem of finding a way to love and be loved by two parents who no longer love each other.

Reactions to loss

The sorrow caused by divorce is different from that following a bereavement, but there are many similarities in the two types of loss. Children feel many of the same emotions—shock and denial, anger, deep sorrow and guilt. There is the added feeling of betrayal; having lost a trusted adult they feel manipulated, and fearful of further loss. Often this starts up aggressive behaviour.

A great deal depends on the ages of the children. Between three and five years they cannot properly voice their feelings of fear, bewilderment and often self-blame, and may show regressive behaviour: suck their thumbs, cling to their custodial parent, wet the bed, sometimes refuse solid food.

Children of six to eight years respond almost identically to children suffering from grief: with crying, sobbing and the tragic signs of yearning and searching for the 'lost' parent.

From nine to twelve, anger is more apparent. They may be hostile towards one or other parent, or both—building up a hate for the parent they see as responsible for the divorce, or towards a foster parent or teacher who appears to condone the whole, awful separation.

Overwhelmed by the helplessness of their situation, many try to reconcile their parents. They become intensely active. This was overheard in a playground: 'If one of us got kidnapped, or was in a car crash, then mum and dad would make it up over our beds—like they do in films!' This is an age when psychosomatic complaints may manifest themselves.

Teenagers can be surprisingly sophisticated in their reactions and express their anger dramatically, either refusing to see one or other parent, or resorting to physical violence—at the same time showing dramatic signs of mental bewilderment in their school work. Younger adolescents are likely to be embarrassed by the divorce, playing truant from school to avoid having to tell their friends. Sudden awareness of their parents' sexuality at a time when older teenagers are preoccupied with experimental relationships themselves, undermines their belief in parental stability. They feel unloved and it hurts. Many will loudly accuse their parents of immoral behaviour.

Others will acquire a responsibility beyond their years and increase in maturity and independence.

Loss of a parent

The loss of a parent is traumatic—especially of a mother. Many psychiatrists talk of mother love in early childhood being as important for mental health as vitamins are for physical well-being. However, there is no evidence that fathers cannot meet this need and bring up their family equally well: in many cases where a mother goes out to work and parental roles are reversed, this is more frequently happening; widowers, whenever possible, become as closely involved with their children as do widows; society is changing its old attitudes and the father is seen not only as the provider of financial security, but of continuous, loving care. Recent research confirms that: 'Fathers as parents on their own are no less successful than mothers on their own.'

Many couples, of course, embark on parenthood with no qualifications other than having been children themselves. They find even one child to be an overwhelming responsibility. When their marriage problems begin, they are quite unable to cope with these as well as with a child—and it is the child who is ignored.

Paula, aged five, was taken to a child guidance clinic because of aggressive behaviour. 'She deliberately cut up her sheets and curtains, she even broke my best china!' Her mother was desperate: 'Paula has inherited violent tendencies from her father!' The clinic discovered that father was violent, but only when mother was having affairs with younger men. There was so much tension in that household, long before the separation, that the little girl was venting her anxiety and need for attention. Actions often explain more than words—yet that mother had no idea it was *her own* behaviour that was affecting her child.

At this stage, many parents are unaware that, for them, divorce is a long-term situation: it will mean that legally they are no longer man and wife but, with a few extreme exceptions, they *are* still father and mother for the rest of their lives. Counsellors today do not always advise couples to remain together, but they do advise them to remain parents in more than name, and to share this lifelong responsibility. 'You will not stop being a father by living apart' one man was told.

The children must be consulted

The Thames Television survey found the strongest factor, throughout their conversations with children, was that parents seldom talk with them, involve them, allow them to be part of the family discussions. Children I have spoken with all want to know what is happening, and to feel their parents respect their wishes and recognize their needs.

A child can sense when things are upset, and fantasies and anxieties will build up in a young mind which can cause far more damage than hearing the truth (see Chapter 2).

The parent–child relationship

Such a relationship is traditionally fraught with difficulty, but if a strong habit of communication between all members of the family can be built up in the children's early years—openness and honesty, with listening as well as talking skills learned—then that will support them all in times of crisis. And divorce *is* a crisis—maybe the most devastating many children have to face.

What the youngsters have to say may well be upsetting, and hurt their parents, but it is far wiser and safer than bottling up all that emotion inside them.

Household routine

The family home will be feeling chaotic even if nothing has physically changed, so it is important to see that routines are kept to: that meal and bedtimes remain the same as usual; that joining in school activities and having friends in to play all continue. There is comfort in the familiar.

Be prepared for conflicting reactions

However carefully you manage to achieve a smooth running of your home, children can be aggressive, uncooperative and demanding. They know something frightening and unpleasant is about to happen which is beyond their ability to alter. How can they prevent it? The only ways they know are either to pretend it will not happen and refuse to listen or talk about any of it; or else to cause so much aggravation and disturbance that perhaps all talk of divorce will go away. Conversely, some children appear callous, or completely disinterested. This could be hiding a deep sadness. There are as many perceptions and reactions as there are children.

Seeking help

Even at this early stage in the long-drawn-out proceedings, parents should not hesitate to seek help. A parent left alone should never try to shoulder the whole burden. A real friend, if possible one who has also been separated, is invaluable—at least they will offer masses of sympathy.

The same goes for the children. Find out which of their friends are also victims of divorce and encourage them to discuss other families' experiences. If possible, *get them to report back to you.* They may hear disturbing stories which will never apply to your family, and pick up ideas that will confuse or frighten them even more than they are already ('Joanna says I will be put into care—does that mean prison, mummy?'). But in many cases, a chat with a friend who has had a similar experience can be comforting.

It is a good idea to tell your doctor what you are contemplating. He may well offer you and your children advice and/or tell you where to seek further help.

Counselling

Counselling is becoming more widely available, and self help groups are now to be found for all types of problems. Caring and advisory organizations are being set up in many countries, quite apart from the professional child psychiatrists and family therapists. Schools will often refer your child to an educational psychologist. Why not take advantage of their expertise and experience?

You may find that each child in your family is reacting to each trauma in a different way, and feel that help or therapy for one will have to differ for another. This is when a counsellor can give you some idea of the types of reactional behaviour to expect, which ones are the more serious, and how much parents and carers can do to alleviate them. Research shows that, no matter how well a child appears to adjust, there is always a period of grief and disturbance.

If parents, before or after they separate, are able to seek advice and handle some of their children's problems *together*, this will pave the way for a journey through divorce with the least possible damage to the family. Happily, the Children Act 1989 has taken up this concept. Arrangements for children can be agreed prior to contact with the Courts, and both parents retain responsibility for them after divorce (see Chapter 4).

2
Telling the Children

Helping a child to understand the reasons for a marriage break-up is a difficult task. A huge event has to be faced with courage and ultimately accepted. Parents, while overwhelmed with their own mixed emotions, have to judge how much of the truth their children are capable of facing. It is usually more than they expect.

Where there is intense acrimony between the parents it becomes even harder, sometimes impossible, for a balanced explanation to be given by both parents together. They vie for their children's love, they exaggerate their feelings of being 'deserted', or they run down the other's character and deride his or her motives.

The youngsters may feel: 'Why should we be dragged into your nasty quarrels?' On the other hand, they long to be included in the discussions and decisions. 'No one asked *us* if we wanted mum to leave.'

Asked by his teacher to write an essay about the most memorable event in his holidays, a boy of twelve wrote of the day his parents told him they were getting a divorce. They sat either side of him and each parent took one of his hands. His father spoke: 'Son, we want you to be the first to know that mummy and I are separating. This may upset you, but the important thing to remember is that we both love you, and always will.' The boy wrote that his father's eyes were filled with tears and his mother was openly crying. 'We both love you,' she echoed. The boy's essay continued with his parents quietly telling him that his father would leave the house and his mother would stay with him. 'But you can go with daddy if you prefer,' his mother said. Both parents were still holding his hands.

'So I let go of both their hands,' the essay ended. 'What else could I do?'

His teacher was moved by the poignant story and certainly I

have not heard such a vivid description of the agonizing conflict of loyalties, the bewildering loss of trust, and the all-engulfing loneliness a child victim of divorce can experience. That essay said it all. His parents probably felt they had handled the problem of breaking the news to their precious only son with intelligent, caring good sense. There is no easy way to tell such news. There is no *right* way.

Family relationships

Much will depend on the relationships in the family prior to the separation. If parents can communicate with their children, and that does not mean only the very articulate, well-educated families—often the opposite is true—then when the most difficult conversation they may ever have to face presents itself they will cope, just by being there, and caring.

Ideally, when marital problems arise, it is preferable to let your children see and hear as little bickering as possible. However, once serious disagreements begin, even small children sense something is wrong ('Mum doesn't kiss dad when he comes home from work any more'). When very young, they react as pets when you are preparing for a holiday: become restless, whine, follow you around until you become exasperated and cross, when they become even more crotchety—and the whole household erupts. Older children soon pick up the atmosphere and rebel, staying out late, refusing to do homework, creating rather than helping with domestic chores.

It is all very well for therapists to advise cool, calm and collected behaviour. Not easy, when your marriage is fragmenting daily. But if parents can remember, during all this depressing time, that their children are actually *suffering*, trying to ease *their* anxieties could help to steady their own emotions.

If a wife is constantly saying unkind things about her husband the children will start to doubt their love for their father—even feel guilty that they love him when their mother plainly does not. In time, their love for their mother may become more a duty than a genuine emotion. Even when a partner has been unfaithful or cruel, it is worth trying to avoid vindictive language. However, never lie to a child and pretend that daddy is a saint, he just had bad luck and is really wonderful. This will only confuse, and make your child wonder why you *want* a divorce.

When love becomes sour, a parent tends to notice all the negative things in a child that can be blamed on her/his partner. 'He's got your temper!' 'She's as mean as her mother!' How distressing for a child to hear such opinions.

A couple who are totally at odds may disagree on how and what to tell the children. One may feel 'the less said the better', while the other wants to talk them through every last detail. Involving another family member, perhaps a well-loved grandparent, a trusted neighbour or teacher, may seem a cowardly way out. But it can help to get a family discussion going.

One child psychiatrist states: 'A child taken into his parents' confidence *as far as his emotional maturity allows*, will recover and adjust to any major change, and will be saved a great deal of stress in the future.'

It may also save him the shock nine-year-old Jenny had last summer:

> The children next door asked me what it was like when parents divorced and I didn't know what they meant. *Mummy hadn't said anything about it.*

Creating the right atmosphere

To be so evasive is cruel—springing it all on them suddenly is grossly unfair, and unwise. 'Next holidays you'll be going to live with mummy and a new daddy in London. Isn't that exciting!' Shocking words for a child to hear.

Without information children cannot understand; with misleading half-truths they will turn to fantasizing. A child may come to believe that his mother despises him, or his father is not proud of him. Above all, he will feel *inferior* because no one considered it worthwhile to let him know the truth about what was going on.

Try not to overburden them with too many explanations, be brief and calm, and let them see the optimistic side of things: perhaps having two homes can be made to sound attractive; perhaps there will be a chance for them to travel if one parent is moving away; they may be allowed a dog now mum is leaving. This may sound trivial, but children like to hear all the practicalities, so try not to let all your news be gloomy. Speak positively, not with anger, trying to instil confidence. 'We hope the arrangements we are considering will help us all.' 'Mummy may be away, but we will manage on our own if we all try hard.'

Where there are several children, it is usually best to tell them all together, so one will not feel that he is being excluded from some of the explanations. Each one may come and ask his own questions later—so give them opportunities to voice their individual worries. Each child should talk with both parents separately, if and when he wants to.

Maybe the family have never talked together about feelings before. Explain that you are ready to share your grown-up thoughts, and listen to the children's ideas, showing that you *care* about their feelings.

Depending on the child's age, take her in your arms, sit her on your lap, or hold her hand. 'Mummy and Daddy have not been getting along well. Have you noticed that? You've heard us arguing/fighting. We feel it will upset all of us to go on living in the same house.'

A teenager may hate to be touched, shake off an arm round the shoulders, but the fact that you are there can reassure her that you care, and that you are not going to leave her—that is what matters. If you have kept things secret up to now, there will be many things adolescents have not fully understood, and you must help them: 'I wonder if you have suspected anything?' will show them you appreciate their intelligence.

Timing is important—never choose bedtime, it may seem cosy and loving, but is she likely to sleep? Just before she is going away is not a good time either, or when starting a new school term.

Philippa, at fifteen, was about to take her first GCSE exams, and two days before the first exam, her parents asked to see the headmistress. 'We are about to get a divorce, we would be grateful if you could tell Phillippa for us,' was the father's opening remark. Horrified, the head tried tactfully to explain that any girl would much rather hear such news from her parents. 'Does she know you are considering this step?' 'No,' replied her mother. 'We did not want to upset her.' Her parents obviously had no conception of how such news could affect a child, and only the educational psychologist could convince them: 'Your daughter must be able to trust you both. You must help her to retain her feelings of personal worth, for she is bound to feel rejected and hurt; you have to do everything possible to boost her self-image and show her your love.'

In a high percentage of families one parent just walks out, or disappears, leaving his/her partner to break the news. Again, never assume children guess—they may suspect, but will still need to be told.

But do not expect a cosy chat. 'I don't believe you, mum. Dad would have told me!'

Barney, at six, asked: 'Why did he leave us?' His granny had to help the distraught mother to reply: 'Maybe he wants to make a new life, I know he did not want to leave *you.* I'm sure he will write or phone us soon.'

What to tell children

Above all, tell them the truth. Never say, for example, 'Nothing will change.' *It will.*

'Dad said mum was having a holiday, but we knew she would never have gone away without telling us.' Tom and Michael *knew* their father was lying, yet never dared to ask him what the truth was. 'I once had a nightmare that she had died,' said nine-year-old Tom.

The truth is usually unpalatable, and many parents choke over the telling of it. Mandy, at fifteen, said her father telephoned her to say he had left home. 'I just hung up, I couldn't speak.'

Children long for truth. Some of them may cover their ears

when they hear it; many become filled with rage; many weep. And beware of no reaction at all—it may lie dormant for many months.

Sadly, parents whose trust in each other has crumbled relate bitter and fictionalized stories to their families:

> Dad told us he had to go to America on business and that mum refused to go with him. Mum said dad had lost his job and was so lazy she had turned him out. We never knew who was telling the truth.

Sometimes, a parent in the midst of the whole messy upheaval will say more than she/he intended. One father, upset by his children's tears, found himself saying that their mother was cruel and did not love them. Afterwards, he regretted this and managed to talk with them again: 'Mummy doesn't love *me* any more, but she loves you children a lot.' Children sense honesty when they hear it, they respond when an adult 'owns up' to a foolish mistake. They feel they have been treated as sensible people, not unthinking babies.

Helping a family

This is when a friend can sometimes help, can confirm a parent's true feelings for his children and give extra assurances to young people that their problems and worries are being considered. It is a difficult message to get across, when the fact that their parents are separating is the one thing none of the children want to happen.

It is hard to talk about painful feelings, and for a child it is hard to describe them. 'I only know they hurt.'

No-one can *pull* feelings from a child, but if a caring adult can coax them out, it is always wise. They may be puzzling and—especially to their parents—be hurtful. But never say: 'You should not be feeling that way,' or, as so many adults do: 'You don't *really* feel that, do you?' If a child says she feels that way, she does. If you can acknowledge that feeling and show you care about it, it will relieve her enormously.

When one parent is obviously—to use the outdated term—the 'guilty' partner, a known and trusted 'outsider' could help break the news. A parent who assumes the responsibility, the guilt (in cases of infidelity, violent or criminal behaviour), is often reluctant to tell the children. Above his own shame will be the guilt he feels on realizing the unhappiness he has, and will in future, cause his children. He has let them down and dreads admitting his failure to keep the marriage going. But in most cases he will want to remain in touch with his children:

> Dad wouldn't talk to us and got our uncle to tell us that mum got a court order to keep dad out of the house. I love my dad and don't see why we can't talk to him. Why can't he tell us himself what he did?

Chris wanted the truth to come from his father even though he knew his mother was unhappy. How could anyone think his feelings would change towards his dad?

Good riddance

There is also the theory that because divorcing parents always feel a share of guilt within themselves, this will relay itself to the children. Self-recrimination is catching.

Liz, only nine, whose dad had physically assaulted the whole family, found it hard to accept her feelings of relief when told about her parents' divorce:

> My brothers said, 'Three cheers and good riddance,' and I joined in, but I felt really bad about it. We all thought they would make it up when we got older. My brothers teased me because I cried, but I hated not being a real family any more. I mean, a family has to have a mother and a father, doesn't it? Mum cried too, I heard her in the night.

Violent homes

In many households, the idea of sitting down in a relatively calm atmosphere and 'telling the children', or even discussing a possible break-up, is unthinkable. The thought of telling 'the truth' would be laughed at. The house has been catastrophic for months, maybe years; it is hard to imagine an emotion such as love ever having existed between the two parents. The children are unused to explanations of behaviour or to any involvement in adult decisions. Youngsters such as Will and Joe do not remember the divorce period as a specific time in their lives:

> We used to hear mum and dad fighting about three or four nights a week. Sometimes we asked mum what it was all about and she said it was nothing to do with us, that we were cheeky to ask about grown-up affairs.

Those boys felt really pained by being left in a child's world, 'as though we couldn't understand anything'. At least they had each other. An only child can feel desperately lonely in such a situation.

In most cases of such continual violence and acrimony, the final break-up, though sudden, is undramatic. A day comes when one parent disappears, and full explanations are seldom given. The parents assume the quarrels to be explanation enough—that the children 'won't really understand anyway'. 'Because I didn't cry, I heard mum telling gran that I'd taken the news well. She didn't see I was numb with shock.'

We both still love you

This is an important message to convey to a child. But it has to be supported by long-term assurances that the love will continue. Pippa was only eight when her parents separated:

> Mum and Papa hugged me and said they loved me just the same as before. But if Papa really loved me, how could he

leave me? It didn't make sense. I knew they must be lying just to be kind to me.

It would be foolish to pretend any of this is easy. Caring parents suffer agonies of remorse, regret, confusion and deep disappointment in their own inability to sustain a relationship; self-recrimination and devastating loss of self-esteem can engulf a wife or husband. On top of this they have to add their fear of hurting their child, of losing their child's love, and shame at being unable to maintain a stable partnership as parents. There is little evidence to show that divorce is ever undertaken lightly—despite the smug comments to that effect by those who have avoided the divorce courts themselves. Almost all separating couples go through long periods, often years rather than months, of anxiety, unhappiness, loneliness and confusion—private misery abounds. This *must* affect the children, even babies.

Conversely, if one parent leaves suddenly, there is equal misery—shock, anger, bitterness, feelings of failure, rejection and isolation, emotional and sexual deprivation, all transmitted to the children. Caring parents' efforts to comfort their families in these circumstances are seldom appreciated.

Maggie's father told his wife and three children, all in their early teens, that he was going to live with another woman. They all cried, or screamed at him, and Maggie remembers hitting him with her fists as hard as she could. Yet she knew that all she wanted was for him to come back to them. 'At fourteen, I seriously thought of committing suicide as I thought then mum and dad would come together again.'

Please tell me why

Child therapists agree that the most common feeling experienced by these children is a painfully confused sadness. A girl interviewed on television said: 'I was kind of old enough to get hurt, but not old enough to understand.'

The basic truth: 'We are getting divorced,' is obviously felt by many parents to be sufficient knowledge to impart to children;

the reasons for the divorce, and the meaning of the changes in parents' behaviour, are never discussed. But experienced child psychiatrists all agree that if a child can recognize her parents have a problem, and are seriously considering divorce as a remedy which will bring relief and a happy outcome for one or both parents—that child will be far better able to cope:

> Dad said: 'Ask your mother,' and Mum said: 'Ask your father.' I don't know if they thought I was too stupid to understand or if they were angry with me. I could see they were angry with each other, but they never told me why.

That plea, *they never told me why*, is repeated over and over.

Particularly sad and stressful for children are homes where problems are never discussed, arguments never heard. There are unwritten but recognized 'rules' forbidding questions on all except trivial subjects. Quarrels are seldom heard, or allowed. When such couples split up, the children can be shattered. The divorce is as shocking as a sudden death—the stress can be extreme.

What words can we use?

Experienced family mediators often get asked by concerned parents what words to use when telling their children. Sometimes, they 'rehearse' this painfully difficult task with the parents. It is, after all, news their children do *not* want to hear. They have to show there is a good reason for the break-up, that they are not acting hastily, or in a fit of temper, or being selfish—but that they have considered it seriously and are still reliable parents. One young teenager's mother said: 'We'll tell you when you're older, you won't understand.' The child replied: 'I don't care if I understand or not, I want you to *tell* me why you're splitting up.'

'If you stop loving each other, you may stop loving us.'

This very natural worry often takes parents by surprise. Now they have to be far more explicit, and in a family where a parent may *never* have said: 'I love you,' to a child, it is especially difficult. Seeds of doubt may already have been sown in a sensitive child's mind. 'Do they love me? They are so full of hate for each other.' How do you interpret the myriad definitions of love to a child?

What about: 'We loved you from the day you were born—that will never stop. Mothers and fathers only meet when they are grown-up, their love *can* change.'

Ask them if they understand what you are saying. They may nod, or mutter 'Yes,' but it is doubtful if they will remember your words clearly for their minds are full of anxieties. It is not enough to 'tell and run'. It needs careful follow-ups and constant involvement with the child. Repeat your words during the next few days, leaving the way open for them to ask more questions.

No need to pour out *all* the complex reasons—how you feel your husband has wronged you, hurt you, rejected you, etc. Your children will then feel obliged to take sides—in this case to side with you which will mean them being against their beloved father. They cannot bear even to think about such a thing. Neil, aged seven: 'If I love dad, will mum stop loving me?'

Even the word divorce needs clarification. The dictionary definition—*Legal dissolution of marriage*—does not explain that to mean a man and woman are husband and wife no longer, but that *they are still a mother and father for the rest of their lives.* Many, many children are never told that important fact. 'We are going to get *un*married,' is a reasonable description for younger children.

It was not your fault

The American film, *Kramer versus Kramer*, which features a 'tug-of-love' custody case, had many heartrending lines. For me, the scene when the eight-year-old boy sobbed into his pillow: 'Mommy left because I was bad!' was the most moving. This was no Hollywood sentiment—it is a deep-felt belief held by very young children the world over: 'I didn't eat my dinner.' 'I'm sorry I wet the bed.'

Surveys show that children from three to seven years are most often left out in terms of explanations from parents. This may well compound their feelings that when something unpleasant has occurred in their world, they must have done something wrong—this is their punishment. Danny remembers a school friend asking him if his mum was divorced. 'I don't know,' he said. 'Well, where's your dad then?' That night he asked his mum: 'Are you and dad divorced?' She said: 'Yes, Danny, get on with your supper.'

Six-year-old David's mother was not home one day when he and his brother returned from school. 'I thought she'd gone because I didn't clear up the mess in my room.'

Whatever else you manage to convey to these little children, you have to make it clear that they are *not* the cause of a parent's disappearance. A young child believes implicitly that even his thoughts can magically cause things to happen. 'I often wished dad would go away when I wanted to watch TV and he sent me to bed, and now he's gone. It's all my fault.'

Even if their fears are unspoken, it is essential to tell children that in *no way* have they caused the family separation. 'You were never bad, you were always lovable, and nothing you could have done would have changed things.' Such assurances need constant repetition—fears and fantasies do not disappear overnight.

Older children seldom feel this guilt, but teenagers can feel a deep sense of responsibility. Jeff (sixteen) said:

> I know I fight with mum all the time. I thought if she and dad let me leave school I could earn some money. They never have enough and my friend says that's the cause of most divorces. It's all because of me that they're so hard up, so that's why they've split up. Mum says it's not my fault, but I know it is. We argue about that now.

Spoken and unspoken questions

Once communications are opened, it must be remembered that children are practical, and will want to know exactly to the last detail what this divorce is going to mean to them—how it will change their lives.

'Where will we live?' 'Will daddy visit us?' 'When?' 'Who will take us to school?' 'Is mummy going to be on the phone?' 'Will granny still want to see us on Sundays?' 'Can the cat come with us?'

They want straight answers, and they want them at once. If arrangements are still undecided, say so. If you are not sure where dad will be living, tell the children.

If the separation means the children have to go into foster care for a while, make sure they know why. 'Because I have to find a flat.' 'Because dad has to be treated in hospital for six weeks.' Never give *vague* answers.

Inevitably, more obtuse questions will follow. 'Why doesn't daddy love us any more?' 'Will you still be my mummy?' Sadly, a parent can be too absorbed in her own anxieties to sense the urgency of the *un*spoken questions: 'Was I so bad that daddy had to run away?' 'If mummy goes away too, will I be an orphan?' Keep on showing, as well as telling tne children that you are still their loving parent.

One father told his sons, when they asked *why* they could not live together again: 'When I'm happy, it's easier for me to make you happy. When I'm unhappy, it's very hard to be the kind of parent you need and enjoy.'

Explain that the separation will prevent any *more* unhappiness and hopefully bring relief, and that you are giving tremendous thought to the best arrangements for *every* member of the family.

'Children are so resilient,' you hear, and in many ways this is true. At all ages, they can be tough, can withstand enormous amounts of stress. But only if they have not lost all sense of security.

Ten years after his mother left home, Peter says:

> Our home was a happy one, and it was hard to imagine it would ever change. Even when mum hinted she might leave, she made it clear that she wasn't divorcing *us*. Dad said that he would try to help us understand more as we grew older. He kept his word and discussed his feelings with us over the years. Our lives changed for ever, but we never felt abandoned or unloved.

Peter was one of the lucky ones—and his is far from the only happy story to emerge from the many and varied tangles that end in the divorce courts. The more children are involved in any family decision-making, the better prepared they will be for making their own, important decisions later in life.

I'd rather not talk about it

His mother could not understand why Ben was so reluctant to go to his friend's house after school, or to visit his grandparents at the weekend. Finally, after two weeks, the nine-year-old boy told his elder brother: 'I don't know what to tell them. Do they know about mum and dad?'

His parents had not thought to tell him that their separation was not a secret, and that he was free to talk or not as he wished. Sometimes a child needs a little help here. He should be warned to expect sympathy, or embarrassment as though it were a death in the family. If a child is too shy to discuss it outside the family, tell him it is perfectly polite to say: 'I'd rather not talk about it.'

Many children feel far more comfortable discussing personal and serious matters with someone other than their parents—maybe someone right outside the family. Never be hurt by this—it is very normal.

Others, like Colin, feel it is wiser to: 'Shut up about it.'

3
After the Break

This period between the decision to separate and the final divorce is one of the unhappiest times for many families. Usually one parent has moved out and the feelings that are now surfacing in the children are similar to those following a bereavement. But there is an added emotion following divorce—their parent has left them voluntarily, rejected them—a devastating belief. 'So that's what adults do!' 'If daddy can walk out on me, so could mummy!' They may cling to the custodial parent, insist on sleeping with her, refuse to be left at school, panic if they lose sight of her in a crowded shop or bus. All this is heartbreaking for parents who have never ceased to love their children and do not wish, ever, to reject them.

Extended families can help during this time, if only to point out to parents that their feelings of anger, bitterness and hurt are not *all* shared by their children unless they instil them into their confused minds. As one grandmother said to her son: 'You may think you are better off without your partner, but the children are not.'

She was right. The very real terror of being rejected can linger into adulthood and affect all their future relationships. A child therapist wrote: 'If a mother has simply vanished from a child's life, this can haunt him all his life; it leaves a large gap in a person's certainty about himself if he has no knowledge of his natural parent.'

Continual contact with *both* parents has been found the safest way to prevent such tragic consequences.

'But how do I know if my child is feeling rejected? He seems fine, and hasn't asked to see his daddy at all.'

Many mothers understandably feel that a counsellor's or therapist's ideas may be academic, and that their children are 'doing all right'. They may well be, but particularly when a mother is longing to be free of her marriage partner and start a new life, she may unconsciously be fooling herself. Even when she sees no outward signs of anxiety, she would be wise to make sure her ex-spouse makes contact, if only by telephone, with his children, *as soon as possible after he has left home.* Try to prevent any feelings of rejection quickly—don't let them grow. Remember, a child may not have asked to see his 'absent' father for fear of upsetting his mother. Anticipating such worries will greatly help your child. This requires great patience on the part of the parent with whom the child lives, especially where there is no extended family to help her out. If you had a happy childhood home yourself, try to imagine how it would feel to be 'let down' by one of the two most precious people in your world.

Where one parent has actually disappeared, or is hesitating over contact, then the parent with whom the children are living *must* seek advice. This is when the mediation services can be tremendously supportive (see Chapter 4).

Feelings a whole family may experience

Mothers usually start to talk about themselves when you ask them about their children. They are concerned about them, of course, but only in terms of what they are *doing*, or *saying*, or how they are *behaving*—seldom do they notice how a child is *feeling.* A family will experience a wide range of emotions, but it is not much use talking about shock, anger, denial, grief and so on—all rather frightening words which have no connection with how a child is feeling deep inside. Obviously every child, every family, is unique—no two reactions are the same. But many families say they would like to have known some of the emotions to expect—to have been told that it is all right to cry, that it is normal to feel angry, sad or afraid.

Shock

This is often the first emotion. A child has suspected things were going wrong, but until the day one parent leaves home, or he is taken away himself, he tries not to believe it. A shortlived feeling of happiness is sometimes felt when verbal or physical fighting stops: that's over, how wonderful. Then guilt creeps in because you feel that way.

Shock can have many effects. A child may appear numb, almost listless and uncomprehending: 'Patsy was so quiet all day, then suddenly the next morning she cried for about two hours.'

Sometimes shock causes physical problems—stomach upsets or vomiting, or an allergic rash. Because of the build-up of stress she has endured, a child may well become prone to infections—catching any cold, cough, ear or eye infection that is around. One child therapist likens such children to puppies separated from their mother for the first time—and suggests that children be treated in the same way. Make bedtime cosy and warm, with hot water bottles, plenty of blankets and lots of reassuring cuddles.

Sadness

Realization that your parent has gone can bring on real grief for a child. Crying, clinging to the other parent, or numb sorrow can result. On top of this lies *anxiety* for the future: will your parent be able to afford to stay in this house? Will it mean moving to a new area, a new school? How will I find new friends? Can the hamsters come with us?

Anger

Anger is one of the strongest emotions to surface. A toddler may throw his toys around the room, a schoolchild kick the furniture or his friends, a teenager resort to vandalism and eventual delinquency. After all, it is only natural to feel anger towards a parent who leaves you. A child often shows anger towards the remaining parent also. 'Why did you make mummy cry?' 'Why didn't you stop shouting at dad, he might have stayed at home?'

A child can be angry with both parents, and then feel cross with herself for not being able to stop them quarrelling. Tension is high, tempers flare, and the whole situation gets out of control.

Nicky was fortunate in having an experienced uncle who saw him and his brothers fighting with their mother after their father had walked out. Uncle took them all swimming, then made them jog all the way home until some of the anger had been knocked away. 'It has to come out,' he said. 'It's never helpful telling children to calm down—the emotions are too deep for that.'

Fear

'If mum stopped loving dad, she may stop loving us.' 'Mum left us, so maybe dad will go away too.'

Some children fear they may be separated from their brothers and sisters. Others fear the parent with whom they are living may die. 'Will dad take us back?' (see Chapter 5).

It is never any good saying, 'Don't be afraid.' Instead, assure the child that you will *never* abandon him. You cannot promise him exactly what the future holds, you may not know yourself—but you can assure him that you will face it together. A child may feel all churned up inside unless she has someone to discuss her fears with. Friends and neighbours can be as awkward as they are following a death: they hesitate to mention the absent parent and make the children feel even more 'different'. This is a time when they need to feel loved and understood; even a kindly smile, or a friendly offer of a lift to school, or a trip to the swings in the park would be reassuring.

Guilt

Guilt is felt by some younger children who feel to blame for their parents' separation. 'I know my parents quarrelled over me.' We have seen (Chapter 2) young children citing their own behaviour. Youngsters need tremendous reassurance of their innocence from an understanding adult. A four-year-old was heard to ask: 'If I'm a good girl, will Daddy come home?'

Above all, children feel confused and rejected. 'Daddy says he loves me, but he's gone to live with that awful lady and not with me. Her children are awful too, so how can he love me?' They lose their trust in one parent, so can they safely trust the other one?

Yet children are seldom heard being disloyal to a parent. They may be rude, aggressive, uncooperative towards the mother or father who they feel has betrayed them—yet if an outsider criticizes that parent, children are fiercely loyal. Billy, whose father was often violent and made their lives miserable, still spoke proudly of: 'Dad, the best darts player in our street.'

Denial

A very strong reaction, one that can persist for many years, is not accepting the fact that the parents have divorced. Fantasies of them being reunited, of all living together again are very strong (although one girl of fifteen was extremely embarrassed to tell her friends when her parents really did remarry each other!). Even after remarriage to a new partner (Chapter 7) children are heard to keep up the hope of a reconciliation. All sorts of ploys are used. Jenny thought if she behaved badly towards her stepmother she would go away and her own mother come back. Tim hoped that if he passed his exams his father would come and live at home again.

These are not unusual feelings, and are often strengthened when one or both parents have themselves not yet been able to accept the reality of their divorce. 'They have not separated emotionally,' as a mediator explained it.

Shame

Many children feel shame, or embarrassment, for there is still a certain stigma attached to divorce—it's a sign of failure, of rejection, of being different. In spite of the statistics, and in some school classes the two-parent families are in the minority (see Chapter 6), there is an initial awkwardness on the part of children to tell anyone that their parents are separating. Tony, fourteen, said, 'It's not the sort of thing to broadcast, but I usually tell people at school if they ask me.'

Friends *do* change in their attitudes sometimes, and relations—especally elderly ones—can be extremely critical instead of sympathetic. Children quickly sense such a climate of disapproval and their mixed emotions are churned up even more inside them.

Physical reactions

Some children develop high temperatures, rashes or stomach upsets. They may not eat or sleep, and develop a stammer or an irritating cough.

At all ages, children can become very difficult. Some deliberately try to be ill. Melanie, still at nursery school, rubbed snow on her tummy 'So I might nearly die and mummy and daddy will cry by my bed in the hospital.' TV influence? Maybe, but that little girl was still desperately unhappy and needed lots of compassionate help.

Less dramatic, but equally distressing for their carers, are the small children who revert to bedwetting, or become disobedient, whining and refusing to sleep at night, tearing their clothes and breaking their toys—which to an already disturbed parent can be the last straw. Many children are, of course, deliberately 'testing' their parents to see how much they can get away with.

I am not suggesting that every child involved in a family breakup will have the same symptoms of stress. One family of three girls whose father left home and quickly remarried had widely varying reactions. The eldest, in her teens, mourned her father as if he had died. The second daughter buried herself in her school work—became an excellent pupil. She says she despises her father and hates his attempts at friendship: 'They're false.' The youngest girl, at ten says: 'He's the only dad I've got, I'm glad we still get to see him.'

Some families appear to have no symptoms. However, the physical and emotional costs of divorce can be high; research shows that a sizeable proportion of these children do show disturbed behaviour at some time. Whether this is due to deteriorating relationships or quarrels prior to the separation, to a child's anxieties and divided loyalties, or to the loss of one parent, is impossible to prove. Many families cope amazingly well, making excellent arrangements to suit their new lives.

Consulting the doctor

If any ailments or problems last for months rather than weeks do make sure a doctor is consulted, who may refer the family to a child guidance clinic. A helpful teacher may suggest an educational psychologist. Parents are sometimes reluctant to admit their children's problems may be emotional ones, and hesitate to seek advice. They feel stigmatized by the divorce, as if they are unworthy of help. Many think it will be an admission of their failure to cope—that their 'care' will be questioned. They also fear they might lose the residential order that allows the children to live with them. On the contrary, their serious concern is a sign of good parenting. So if you are a friend, *do* insist they seek advice.

Different ages, different needs

Children's ages at the time of the family break-up must be taken into account when arranging their futures. Remember, too, that each year will bring them new understanding—and with it new anxieties, fresh problems. However much a parent wishes to leave the past behind, a child will need constant 'updating' on family affairs.

The early years

During the first three years of life every infant demands a continuous relationship with a parent figure—not necessarily the biological mother or father, but a *special* person. From this secure beginning, many professionals say that a basis is formed for all future relationships that a child will make—within the family, at school, at work, in marriage and with his own children.

So a break with this early attachment can affect a child's life. One child and family psychiatrist goes so far as to say that, 'The loss of a parent's interest causes a child to feel valueless and bad.' This may explain extreme clinging to his main carer, thumb-sucking, bedwetting and tantrums.

Several recent studies show that children from five to nine years are most affected by their parents' separation. Their home and family are still the most important part of their lives. From eight years onwards, they try to understand, to work things out for themselves, but the reasons behind their parents' actions are confusing. Boys seem even more disturbed than girls at this age; they tend to show real sadness—crying a lot, yearning for the absent parent, desperately afraid to find out what will happen to their home, their security. Their eating and sleeping patterns often become disrupted.

Ten to twelve-year-olds begin to show anger, or manage to avoid situations—often denying what has happened. Roger was ten when he told his granny, 'Mum is only living away from us for six months.' In fact, his mother was planning to remarry and had told Roger many months before. By denying this, the child perhaps felt it would not actually happen.

Teenagers

No studies can dismiss the fact that during adolescence a child may well begin to change his/her behaviour. He wants to try out his independence, to show his parents he can manage alone, and this often results in wild, irrational and disruptive behaviour.

It is easy to put the blame on a divorce. Teenagers may well leave home when it becomes a troubled place—and some turn to having several sexual relationships in a sort of search for love. 'Mum's having love with that young man,' is an excuse for promiscuity. Dad is no longer there to be a role model or provide discipline—his teenagers are left confused and feel badly let down.

I feel it is important for children to know that at *some* time, their parents loved each other, and had good times, even if later on things went wrong. Otherwise, what are they being told? That all men are horrid and unreliable, their mother is a victim; or that all women are unfaithful and their father is being deserted? That they are the miserable accidents of pure, loveless lust?

'That's idealism,' said Liz, the victim of a man who abused her both mentally and physically. That may be—but Liz's doctor advised her *not* to say, 'Your father is despicable and that's why we don't visit him.' He suggested she told them he was ill.

'Explain that his illness, whether alcoholism or violence, means you are all leaving him for safety. In that way they will not feel guilty, and not hate their father.' He was right: hate is *not* an easy emotion for anyone, let alone a child, to live with.

On the whole, teenagers are less seriously affected in the long term than their younger brothers and sisters. They have had a few secure years (even in an acriminonious household they have been ostensibly a normal family), and they are beginning to know what adult relationships are about. They will soon be living independently of their parents. If they are lucky enough to have parents who talk with them, and treat them as young adults, they can, and do, cope extremely well. It is sad when their childhood years have to end abruptly, but they may well gain in maturity by their experience.

We want to know what is going on

Simon, eleven, and Rachel, twelve, were very troubled, longing to know what was going on after their father left home. They heard their mother talking on the phone about making wills and signing legal decrees; they wanted to know where their father was, and longed to help their mother. 'She seems to forget we're dad's children.'

Twelve-year-old Colin also wished his parents had talked more:

> Mummy and Daddy were very calm about deciding who should have the furniture and the things in the house and mummy wrote it all down and suddenly my brother, he's seven, began to scream. He thought they had to decide who would have *him*. He said he didn't want to be on anyone's list, and he didn't want to live in a house with no beds and chairs in it either.

Conversely, Louise's parents were using her as *their* parent. They poured out their problems to her, expected her to look after the younger children, and often let her stay home from school. 'They seem to think I'm twenty, they forget I'm *nine*!'

Helping children to talk

'How do you feel?' is not the best opening, usually extracting an exasperated, 'I don't know.' Yet a child's feelings may be so strong they frighten her. Asking her if she feels anger, denial, grief or guilt—using all the words a teacher might describe as *non-active*—is not much use. Understanding adults talk about some of their own feelings. In one family, everyone seemed to use the right tactics:

Granny said: 'I feel very cross and angry today, do you?', and her grandsons of ten and thirteen were surprised. 'You see, I love your mummy and daddy and I'm cross that they're separating and messing up the family.' Those boys were then free to express their own anger and not feel shy to admit it.

Meanwhile, granddad suspected they felt somehow to blame, partly responsible, but guilt was far too serious a word. 'It's not anyone's fault about mother and father, lads. I'm sure it's not mine, and it's certainly not *your* fault.'

It was left to the boys' older sister to handle their grief. 'I feel terribly *sad* on some days, really sad all over, do you? I suppose it's because there's nothing we can do about the divorce. Does that make sense to you?' The boys began to talk. Yes, they felt sad, they felt helpless, they felt things were happening in their lives over which they had no control. They poured it all out and found great comfort in being together.

Helpful friends

If adults can provide that sort of mutual help to children and allow them to feel old enough to be confided in, this gives children tremendous confidence. Too often, well-meaning friends or relations rush in with thoughtless remarks. 'Do behave, this is much harder for your mother than it is for you.' Young boys are told: 'You are the head of the house now!' This is *not* a good idea, unless it comes from the child. Understandably, he will feel resentful: 'That's dad's job, he should be here.'

Colin's aunt kept telling him, 'Your mummy is unhappy, be

kind to her.' 'What about me?' he asked, 'I'm unhappy too.' Even when acknowledging a child's sorrow, an adult sometimes thinks a present will make things better. 'As though an ice-cream could stop me feeling depressed!' said Colin.

If you are a parent, try to put yourself in your child's shoes. Were *your* parents divorced? If so, you must recall some of the feelings—so *tell* your child about them. 'I remember feeling very angry, are you?'

Watch for signs of anxiety too, which may show in sucking a thumb or twisting their hair, or continually feeling sick. Sometimes ignoring a tantrum stops it, but finding out what *causes* it is best. Merely to shout, 'Stop it!' is seldom any use. To an overwrought mother, one psychiatrist said: 'If you hassle your children less and find out what's really bugging them, you would begin to get along with them.'

Children, as well as adults, frequently become clumsy when their minds are in turmoil—breaking things or tripping over. Try to put them at ease, perhaps saying: 'I broke a cup today, it must be catching!' Never admonish them, which may make them believe they *are* clumsy—a label which could stick in their minds for years. As much physical activity as possible is good, strenuous games in the garden, races or climbing trees. In the house, helping to paint a room or clear out a cupboard—anything to keep them active and allow some physical aggression to be used up.

Most parents will know other families who are separated, although telling everyone is not a good idea. Advice is free, and as such is thrown about all too liberally—most of it conflicting, some of it harmful. Talking with a close friend, finding out how her children are behaving, and who or what is helping them, is of real value. Can she recommend a doctor? Are the school teachers sympathetic?

Sharing experiences can be of great value—and in Britain there are a growing number of self-help groups for separated parents. Many include special play-groups, discussion sessions or outings for the children—and in the early days of a family break-up these can be invaluable. It takes courage for the first few times, and the children may grumble all the way there—but often it becomes one place where everyone can relax.

4
How the Law can Help your Children

Since the Children Act 1989 was implemented in October 1991, the whole process of divorce for families has altered. The emphasis of this comprehensive and far-reaching reform of child law in Britain is on the rights of children to be heard *and listened to*, and on encouraging parents to reach agreement on children's arrangements without the courts having to get involved. What happens is that one parent completes a 'Statement of Arrangements for Children', which can be sent to his/her partner *before* the divorce process begins. Only when parents cannot reach an agreement on their child's future will the courts need to be involved and a judge called on to give his view.

Court Welfare

If a couple does get to the stage of court proceedings (through disagreements concerning their children), most courts will wish to investigate whether the dispute can be resolved through mediation. There will usually be a preliminary hearing at which the couple may be asked to see a court welfare officer, who will explore the possibility of mediation either through the Court Welfare Service or a local out-of-court service. If mediation does not settle the dispute, a different Court Welfare Officer will prepare a report to help the court decide matters.

Mediation services

Mediators, family solicitors and the courts themselves now agree that it is highly desirable for parents to sort out their difficulties without ever going to the courts. Mediation (in some cases still known as conciliation) helps separating couples do just that.

Mediation services will, in fact, be the key element of the new Family Law Act, 1996, due to come into force in about three years' time. It is hoped that pilot studies on all aspects of the Act will lead to further improvement in the legal climate for effective mediation.

This means helping parents manage the *whole* divorce process *together*, in the interests of their children. Already, mediators have a huge role to play in keeping communication open between parents, so that bitterness will not continue (often through second marriages) and upset the children. A spokesperson for National Family Mediation (NFM) considers that 'Mediation is in accord with the principles of the Children Act in that it values and supports parental responsibility—working towards each parent carrying out that responsibility co-operatively after the divorce.'

NFM is one of the two main organizations providing out-of-court mediation services, the other being the Family Mediators Association (FMA). Both are registered charities; fees will vary according to circumstances. Hopefully, by the time the new Act is implemented, many more services, backed by the necessary funding, will be available. Other organizations are now offering mediation training, prominent among them being the Solicitors Family Law Association (SFLA).

National Family Mediation deals primarily with children's issues, while the FMA offers comprehensive (now more commonly called 'all issues') mediation, where an experienced family lawyer mediator, and a mediator with a background in social work and/or counselling, will usually work together at all sessions, and will deal with both money and children's issues.

Mediation services are basically a way to help families focus on the future. Parents are spoken with in their roles as father and mother, *not* man and wife. NFM explain that they do not focus on how parents *feel* but on what they are going to *do*. They acknowledge the couple's mental turmoil, and they know that no amount of mediation or advice can prevent a child recognizing, and suffering from, bitter conflict between her parents. So the questions they ask are practical ones: 'What is your separation going to mean for your children?'; 'What arrangements are you going to make for their future?'

Mediation is not therapy, but the results can be therapeutic. It offers support, helps couples negotiate ways to reach agreement over arrangements for the children. This gives mum, dad *and* the children the opportunity to hear and understand each other's point of view in a neutral setting. Most importantly, it can guide parents towards understanding the needs of their children.

Family lawyers and mediators agree that it is important for clients to have access to independent legal advice before, during and after mediation, as well as when mediation is inappropriate or breaks down. They stress that legal advice and mediation are not mutually exclusive, but rather should be seen as complementing each other.

Families usually have about three or four one-hour to one-and-a-half-hour sessions. Often these enable parents to see how seriously their behaviour is affecting their children; and many youngsters come to understand that no stigma attaches to them if their parents divorce, and that they are normal if they feel angry. Most of all, they can see that both their parents are concerned about them and are taking steps *together* to deal with their future welfare. This can effectively prevent children from playing one parent against the other, which so often happens when they always see their parents *apart*.

Mediation does *not* mean counselling. However, some mediators, who understand only too well the bewilderment of children trapped within a divided household, are planning to include child counselling (with parental consent) in the service. Mostly, they try to work through the parents, but when they sense a family needs particular help, sometimes a talk with an understanding mediator might be of greater comfort to a vulnerable child than whisking her off for more formal professional counselling.

Many couples turn to mediation services again *after* their divorce. Arrangements may need revising as the children get older and more independent, or if a stepfamily is causing fresh complications.

Legal language

Many of the legal terms used during divorce proceedings prior to the Children Act 1989 were highly disturbing to children, particularly when not fully explained. Happily, such words as *custody* and *access* are no longer in use. But clear explanations of the language still need to be given to all children:

Parental responsibility

Each parent retains parental responsibility for the children after divorce, which responsibility both are entitled to exercise independently of the other, whether living with or apart from their children. This means that mother *or* father may give consent to medical treatment, make decisions on important matters such as change of schools, religion and so on.

*Un*married fathers do not automatically have parental responsibility, but can achieve it in several ways: a) if they get a residence order; b) they apply independently for a parental responsibility order; c) they make a formal agreement with the child's mother without having to go through the courts at all.

No order principle

Parents are now encouraged to make their own arrangements concerning the children, the courts only intervening where there is disagreement or a child may need protection. One legal mediator explained: 'If the court is satisfied with the arrangements made by the parents, the only order that would be made is that *no* order has to be made!'

If, however, no agreement can be reached, the Act provides the courts with a flexible range of orders:

Residence order

This is an order settling where and with whom the children are to live. This could be with a member of the extended family (see Chapter 8). No matter who the order is in favour of, neither parent loses parental responsibility.

Contact order

The order or arrangement made for children to see the parent they do not live with. Details of such visits can be left to the parents, or specific times, places and frequency can be written into the contact order.

As a family child psychiatrist says: 'Successful management of contact is the single most important factor in reducing to a minimum emotional upheavals for children.'

These early arrangements may well need the help and cooperation of family and friends. Emma's (aged ten) upset when her father left home was made worse by her mother's extremely emotional state. She refused to see her father, so her school friend's parents decided to 'step in'. Whenever Emma visited them, they talked about her father, described his new home, explained that he often had meals with them and that he was missing her very much:

> I still felt angry at daddy for upsetting mummy, but curiosity overcame me, and I met him with my friend for Sunday lunch. He was the same, loving daddy, but I was scared to tell mummy. Then my friend's parents told her and she agreed it was all right so long as *I* wanted it. Now I can love them both again.

Ideally, if parents live near each other, visiting times can be frequent, sometimes flexible, and *seen to be approved* by the parent the child lives with. Grandparents often come into their own here, offering a 'neutral' ground for visits. However, in reality many children are collected and delivered like parcels on appointed days, and heaven help the parent who does not deliver on time!

Sharon, aged nine, lived with her mother, who had agreed to take her to her father's home every Saturday morning. Each week the little girl cried on arriving, then again on leaving. Every time the parents argued as to who was frightening the child, until eventually Sharon told her grandmother: 'Mummy doesn't want me to see daddy, she says he ought to be punished for leaving her.' So often one partner, who did not want the divorce, has a deep fear of being alone and cannot see how much sorrow she is causing her child.

Perhaps the only people who can help a parent, and thereby his or her children, to face these problems, are those who have experienced divorce themselves. There are self-help groups of divorced and single parents around the country, notably Gingerbread (see Sources of Help), who will provide friendship and support. 'Since joining I've met so many others in my position—they were able to warn me how emotional we would all feel over contact visits.'

As the months and years go by, there is always the danger of the absent parent moving away, or one parent remarrying and cutting all contact. But there is also a good chance that the whole family will adjust to the two homes and make visits more flexible, dad taking the children for haircuts or to the dentist, mum continuing to take them to visit grandma. Perhaps Colin, 12, sums up what is not an unusual situation:

> Who cares what any of the court orders say? All we worry about is how mum behaves when we visit dad, and how long she lets us stay before ringing up and being a bore.

Yes, many mothers are left with the dirty washing, the meals to cook and the squabbling youngsters after 'a smashing weekend' with dad. But not every absent husband is a wealthy philanderer—many are trying hard to become better fathers than before in the precious hours allotted to them.

When contact is denied

> I want desperately to carry out my parental duties and responsibilities to my three children whom I love dearly. How dare their mother deny them their *right* to see me.

Yes, it is the children who have *right* of contact with an absent parent. In practice, however, there are no real sanctions if a mother refuses to cooperate. No court willingly sends a mother to prison for breaking a contact order, because of the effect on her children. So she can move away, or simply refuse to allow her children to visit their father. 'They don't *want* to see him,' she may tell the court.

Why is contact so wilfully denied? Why would a mother seek to destroy her children's relationship with their father? There are tragic instances of caring fathers who have not seen their children for many years. It is not hard to imagine the psychological effects this lack of contact with both parents can have on a child. Whatever the parent they live with has told them, they will feel abandoned by one natural parent.

This feeling may be well grounded—many fathers either forget, or cancel, their visits even while a frantic mother is doing her best to give her children every opportunity to be with their father. Before parental responsibility was implemented, around half of 'absent' fathers lost all contact with their children after two years.

But the opposite can happen. Mothers, embittered by memories of an unhappy marriage, can 'brainwash' their children until they truly don't want to see their fathers, ever again. When adults, they may wish to find out the facts for themselves, but the damage will have been done—their childhood will have lacked one important person.

Specific issue order

If there is one particular issue regarding a child on which the parents disagree, the court may be asked to resolve the matter by making a specific issue order. An example of this would be one parent wanting the child to go to a different school.

Prohibited steps

A court can also make an order preventing someone from carrying out a particular course of action in relation to a child. During court decisions involving any of the above orders, the interests of the children are paramount. They will always be given an opportunity to voice their opinions and declare their wishes. Often, a Court Welfare Officer will talk with a child and be able to pass on their views to the court. Many social workers also seem to have taken on board the concept of children *being listened to*. This means they now work far more closely with parents over arrangements for the children, and have recognized that in many cases extended families (especially grandparents) can be a great help with all the complex decisions to be made.

Children's applications

Once they have applied to the court to do so, and are acknowledged to be 'of sufficient understanding', young persons can make their own applications to the court. Under the Children Act they can apply for orders laying down where they will live, who they will see, or deciding any other questions relating to their upbringing.

Maintenance

Following divorce, both parents are financially responsible for their children. Since April 1993 a section of the Department of Social Security, the Child Support Agency (CSA), has dealt with the assessment of child maintenance payments. The CSA will become involved automatically if the parent with whom a child usually lives is in receipt of certain state benefits such as income support or family credit. Alternatively, an application can be made by one of the parties to the Agency. However, courts can still make orders in many cases, and it is often worth seeking legal advice on the best course of action. The CSA cannot deal with maintenance for stepchildren, cases where either of the parties of the child is abroad, or cases where there is already a formal agreement between the parents or a court order bearing on maintenance (except where one of the parents starts receiving state benefits). CSA offices around the country can also answer your queries. The National Council for One Parent Families also issues a comprehensive guide on the subject (see Sources of Help).

Bitter arguments over finance seldom escape the notice of children.

> Whenever dad comes to pick us up, mum goes on and on about his contributions to our support. She makes us feel guilty and dad gets angry. I dread weekends.

Because contact visits may be the only time after a divorce that parents meet, there is a good chance they may use them to air their grievances. This is one reason why contact often lessens, then finally falls away over the first year or two. A father may feel he is 'disturbing the children'; a mother may feel so guilty about 'abandoning' them that she prefers to disappear completely.

Stolen children

The Foreign and Commonwealth Office estimate that over 1,000 children are abducted from Britain each year and taken overseas—mostly during or following marital separation. With the divorce rate going up and European barriers coming down, they fear this number will continue to increase.

These are not always the horrendous 'child snatchings' depicted in the media. The Children's Legal Centre says they frequently represent deep feelings of frustration. The father or mother concerned may be genuinely afraid for the child's welfare and safety; they may be desperate at legal delays. But the trauma for the other parent, and in many cases for the small child taken from familiar surroundings and loving families, can be heartbreaking. Lucy, now fifteen, was abducted at the age of five by her father, returned a year later, then taken away again when she was eight. She is now back with her mother, but says: 'I still have nightmares about flying, and think every day might be my last with mother. I stay with her now, I don't go out with my school friends.' A consultant psychiatrist says that Lucy still suffers from a high level of anxiety and finds concentration on her school work very difficult.

But it has to be said that several children, usually over the age of eight, have *not* seen their abduction as a 'kidnapping' but as 'going on holiday' with daddy or mummy. Some children even look on it as an adventure. One brother and sister were taken from their school playground by their father and lived with him in Italy for a year. When their mother finally came to take them home they were very confused. 'I remember being worried on both occasions, but never frightened,' says Keith, and his sister adds: 'We just wished our mummy would let us love our daddy.'

The law in this country takes an extremely dim view of parents who remove children from the jurisdiction of the other parent, and will do everything in its power to bring those children back. Kidnapping is a criminal and extraditable offence. But the implementation involves a lengthy, difficult and often costly procedure, and in many countries (even within Europe) an impossible one. Sadly, until governments recognize each other's decisions, abduction will continue to pay.

It is important for all parents to have a solicitor who has the experience and the office resources to act effectively in an emergency. Tragic stories appear in the press of 'tug-of-love' babies—although, as one distraught mother remarked, 'There is not much *love* involved.' Resentment and pride and, worst of all, retaliation, are usually at the root of each sad affair.

Many children try to remain loyal to both parents. When parents are so bitter towards each other that they can deprive their own child of one natural parent, perhaps for years, they surely do not deserve any children and certainly not their loving loyalty.

'Religious divorce'

It is possible for parents to separate and go through a form of 'religious divorce' or annulment of marriage, which is recognized within their own religion. The most usual are either 'Catholic annulment' or Islamic '*talaq*' divorce. For those following

Orthodox Judaism, a '*get*' has to be obtained from the court of the Chief Rabbi before remarriage can take place.

In all situations, legal advice is essential. On applying to remarry, a British resident has to have a final decree that is recognized in this country.

Where marriage partners have different nationalities, it is even more urgent for them *to seek professional advice* if they wish to separate and make arrangements for their children. Orson's father came from London and his mother from Nigeria. When they divorced, and he went to live with his mother, he said to the mediator: 'It's hard enough to know I have to leave my father, but it means I have to leave the white part of me also. I feel as if I'm only half a boy now.'

Adoptive parents

Adoptive parents have all the responsibilities and duties of natural parents. Sometimes their children worry that their parents' separation may cause them to be abandoned. They need very active assurances that they *still have two parents*.

5
Living in Two Homes

A *two-home* family is surely a far happier, and more accurate, description of a divided home, than a one-parent family. It also differentiates between families where only one parent is acknowledged, or ever appears. At its best it can, and often does, work well for children. 'I've got a town house and a country house and two bedrooms, and two toy cupboards.' Mercenary? Maybe, but also very practical, and for those able to maintain such an arrangement, a positive approach can only be good. Once divorce is a fact, it should be accepted, and all efforts made to rebuild relationships *within the new situation* of parents living in separate homes.

Preparing for separation

Of all children under ten 60 per cent have to face a move as well as a loss of one parent. So how do you prepare them?

Six-year-old Paul had to leave his home, his school, his friends, one set of grandparents, as well as his adored daddy. His mother had to move back to her parents' home where she could find work, and his granny could fetch him from school each day. To lessen the trauma, Paul's father moved with them, stayed on for a few weeks, got to know the new neighbourhood and school, met Paul's new friends, and showed his son that he was still very much a part of his life. The plan eased Paul's anxieties, and he accepted the truth from his parents: 'We are much happier apart, so long as we can both see plenty of you.'

Another father took his two daughters of eight and ten to visit their grandparents and say goodbye before they moved to another town after their mother left home. He explained they could come back to stay in the holidays, and also helped them to arrange visits with their school friends. As Jenny said, 'It was hard saying goodbye, but better than being whisked away with no explanations and no chance to cry.' Wise words from a ten-year-old.

Life is never the same again

The children are now living with *one* parent; let us assume this to be the mother. No matter how carefully she has assured them of their father's love and concern, and how frequently they are in contact with him, life is different from now on. As many children say: 'Life will never be the same again.'

For a parent to deny this would be foolish. Counsellors suggest replying: 'Yes, you are right. But it does *not* mean that things will be *worse*. In time, they may even be *better*.'

This positive talking is extremely difficult for a depressed and lonely mother but using it can cheer herself as well as her children. When Peter said, 'Christmas and birthdays will never be the same,' his mother replied: 'No, you'll probably get *two* Christmas and birthday parties now!'

A mother may feel unsure if she is able to cope now she is living alone with the children; or she may sense that they really want to stay with their father, and are staying with her out of pity. Either way, she is in a very vulnerable state, emotionally, in which to face the hard task ahead. The legal process is ended, but the *emotional divorce* is far from over.

A lone parent will be viewed with suspicion by neighbours—often expected to have troublesome children. This is where sensitive friends and relations can step in and help the children to make new friends and get to know the local sports centre, library or youth club. Like bereavement, divorce can be isolating. All of which is compounded by the fact that most people no longer live near relatives and childhood friends, so that they are seldom surrounded by a network of kinship within walking distance. A housing estate in a big city can be lonelier than a remote country cottage.

Financial difficulties

It is seldom just a case of dad or mum moving out of the matrimonial home. Often this has to be sold, so that both homes are new. There is much evidence that a considerable proportion of divorced families are likely to suffer financial hardship, if not actual poverty. In Britain, the National Council for One-Parent Families give tragic statistics: 'The divorced and separated in Britain make up over 60 per cent of all lone parents, a high percentage of whom receive state benefits.' Certainly divorce, in the majority of families, causes a lowering in the standards of living and increased economic insecurity. This can have a serious effect on children, not merely in their materialistic expectations ('Why can't we have new bikes/a holiday/meat every day?'), but also on their physical and mental health ('Mum has to work, she's never there in the holidays').

There is no doubt that the shortage of money, even the fear of shortage, can cause tension, bitterness and resentment. When you are trying to care for disturbed and unhappy children, this heightens the misery, which in turn reflects on the whole family.

According to your children's ages, discuss money matters *with* them. 'Yes, we will walk and not take the bus today. We're saving up for your new calculator.' Of course, limitless money will not ease hurt feelings of rejection and deprivation of love—but it does ease one fear, and in practical terms can give a solid stability in home, in social contacts, and in any therapy that needs to be paid for. Sadly, in some areas, this is a need.

Children desperately need reminding that they are not just another complicating factor which their overburdened mother would be better off without. 'Where children are involved, you can't possibly make a clean break.' Jim and Kathy heard their mother saying this and felt guilty that they were *in her way*. A mother trying to keep up her contributions to help support her child is very vulnerable ('But everyone at school has a leather jacket, mum!'). If there are feelings of bitterness towards her ex-husband, they will constantly resurface. A mother can resent having to depend on a man she no longer loves, or one that she despises, or is angry with. This feeling tells on her children.

Acting as go-between

Frank meets his dad one evening each week after school. He is sixteen now, but still cannot bring himself to tell his mother that his father always asks after her: 'Mum *never* asks how dad is.'

Too much pressure can be put on a child whose parents continually criticize each other. In all innocence a young child can pass on remarks, not necessarily meaning to hurt, but out of a frantic desire to please one parent. A child may repeat words the other one has said—causing even greater rifts and losing some of the friendship of one parent.

Contact

The word *contact* (the act or state of touching; the state or fact of communication) has a dauntingly businesslike sound to a parent suddenly separated from his or her children, although it is less harsh than the old term of *access* (meaning approach, or right of entrance). In the US it is called *visitation*, which surely turns the children into visitors rather than family. No legislation can adequately describe a child's natural wording for this most *un*natural situation: 'Let's go and see daddy.'

How the contact is handled, by both parents, varies in every family, and often changes in significance as the children grow older. But recent research cannot be overlooked when the findings reveal that:

(1) Children who continue to have good, continuing relationships with both parents are the least affected by separation.
(2) Children of openly conflicting parents, whether separated or not, are affected quite seriously.
(3) Children who never see the parent they do not live with, usually the father, are the most emotionally disturbed of all.

The early days of meetings with, or visits by, the parent who has left home are the hardest. It feels strange seeing your father or mother in a new home, perhaps a bedsit or shared accommodation, and knowing that you only have half a day with him or her. It requires a lot of work on the part of the parent to establish a calm, natural atmosphere—not always feeling obliged to take the children on exciting outings, or buy them expensive new toys or clothes. Father should never be looked on as Father Christmas.

Small children can play quietly with the special toys or books they keep in 'daddy's place'. Teenagers sometimes take turns to choose an outing. Ideally, the parent lives in the same area or town—then the whole operation is less traumatic, and as they get older they can walk or cycle there on their own.

Problems arise when a family consists of a wide range of ages. Your eleven-year-old son and fifteen-year-old daughter will not always want to go on the same outings or even watch the same TV programmes, and their six-year-old sister will want far more attention than either of them. If different times can be arranged for their visits, it will work far better. Perhaps friends could be asked to join them:

> Dad never lets me bring my friends to his place, it makes me feel as if I ought to be ashamed of it and I'm not.

Also, each child needs time to be alone with that parent—not necessarily for long, heart-to-heart discussions—but to get comfortable with each other, so that they can feel closer.

Each child must have a special place, if not a room, for their things. Dan has a garden shed and that is very special. 'I keep my cricket bat there and an old steam engine kit I work on with dad.'

Contact centres

In many cases, where a father is violent, or a mother mentally disturbed, and any contact at all seems a threatening situation, a court welfare officer can arrange visits within a pre-arranged place (often called a *Saturday Centre*) where the parent with whom the children are living can take them and hand them to the officer, who will accompany them to a room where the other parent is waiting. The 'other' parent may well feel this is like a prison visit, but it would be sad if such an arrangement was turned down. Playing with a small child, talking with an older one, perhaps just reading or playing cards together, will keep up the all-important contact. In time, things may well change—and once trust is built up it may be possible for freer visiting.

For parents who wish never to meet, it is often the only way to arrange contact. For children, it can become a weekly 'treat' where they meet parents and perhaps brothers and sisters for a few hours' play. Sadly, it can also be an insight into family relationships that have never, and never will, be anything other than acrimonious for parents and heartbreaking for children.

Linda, aged nine, came in with her foster mother to meet her natural mother who had agreed to take her out to Macdonald's. Linda, in clean white socks and a clean dress, waited—and waited. Her mother never came. No tears, she had obviously been let down before, but there was a coldness in that little girl's eyes and she snatched a toy away from another child before she left.

Steve, on the other hand, was waiting for his father who, though he had to travel nearly 200 miles for his three-hour weekend visit, was well on time and gave his son a wonderful morning.

Emma, only four-and-a-half, was crying when left by her mother who said loudly. 'I don't want to see that awful man, thank you.' A Centre helper played with the little girl while her father sat quietly beside them reading from a story book. After nearly two hours, Emma crept up onto his lap. It took several visits before she would play alone with her father—but without the patience of the Centre's staff she might never have made contact.

So many goodbyes

How do you cope with the partings every time? This is a hard one. It is sometimes used as an excuse by a reluctant parent to curtail visits, or to stop them altogether. 'It's too upsetting for the children.'

But they are upset because they love that absent parent—no other reason. Why not acknowledge that and assure them that in time they will get used to these frequent partings. Divorce is bad enough for a child without suffering the *total* loss of a loved parent.

When the children are still toddlers, many fathers after a visit take the youngsters home and put them to bed. This way they become very much a part of their lives and so parting is not a problem.

This may sound idealistic for many parents—still too hurt and embittered to have any contact with their ex-spouse. But once they can 'separate emotionally' from each other, and only communicate on a parental level—then they will find that the lifting of bitterness will make all arrangements much easier. They may have failed as partners, but they can still be united as parents.

'After all,' said one twice-divorced mother, 'it's such a joy to have someone actually wanting to take the kids away for a few hours every so often, I think I'm very lucky.' Wise philosophy.

There are other mothers who cannot share her feelings. For them, perhaps living on a new estate, the children are their whole lives—they hate it when they are away, even for an hour, and resent their ex-partner coming anywhere near their home.

There is also the very real fear on the part of some of those parents whose children are living with them, that the residence order arrangements might be reversed—that something they do or say might give the 'absent' parent grounds to make a fresh application for a parental responsibility order. Mediators can often help in these cases: 'The more frequent and amicable contact an ex-husband has with his children, the more likely he is to keep up his financial contribution to the household.'

There are many connotations of the whole worrying subject; but in every case the final outcome always hinges on the fact that contact with both parents is the best solution in the circumstances.

Living with mother

Mothers often have to survive harsh comments. Jean's husband left her with two small sons. 'Of course you know they'll grow up queer,' said a colleague at work. Other hints from teachers and social workers through the years suggested they might become disturbed, deranged and ultimately delinquent.

Immediately after separation, both parents usually experience depression, which will cause intense anxiety, sorrow and anger. They feel inadequate and often become physically ill. Just when their children are in the greatest need of support, loving care and attention, mothers can be too wrapped up in their own mental and physical ailments to notice that Frances has developed a stammer or Penny has become very aggressive towards her friends. However, you will be no use to them as a depressed and unhappy parent. Depression is contagious—the longer it lasts the more vulnerable the rest of the family become. A girl of fifteen: 'Mum never goes out and has fun, it makes me feel so guilty when I do.'

To help children it is important to keep as many familiar routines as possible—normal meal times and bed times, continuing activities as before, visiting grandparents regularly. If they live in the same neighbourhood as before and attend the same school, that is reassuring. Children hate change.

Friends can help, but not always by taking the children 'off the parents' hands' (this can happen too frequently when they are living with father). Remember that the children have 'lost' one parent and will be over-anxious for the other one—they need to be at home to feel 'safe'. Join in the chores around their house, or take them some snacks and watch TV together. Teenagers will appreciate discussion of homework—perhaps the loan of a book, or the use of a home computer. A mother on her own inevitably makes friends with others in the same situation, and a household can become excessively female. Good supportive networks in the community tend to provide the most help for newly separated families, and children cope best when encouraged to socialize and bring friends home.

The absent parent

Meanwhile, the children will be missing their absent parent. 'Will dad be looked after?' 'Is mum lonely?' If distance allows, it is helpful if they can see the absent parent's home as soon as possible after the break-up.

'Will dad still take me to football?' Jack (eleven) asked his mother the day they moved into a new flat. She thought his request selfish, but Jack's Saturday football was part of his life. He was losing so much, he wanted to hang on to anything that he could. There is comfort in the familiar—one of the things divorce does away with.

Teenagers

At one divorce counselling session, every aspect of divided homes was discussed. One mother felt her children were well able to cope with the separation. However, in the *teenage only* group, daughter Mandy had her say:

> Mum took me to stay with granny for Christmas and I had a good time until I realized that she and dad had split up. It shook me. Gran told me he was living with a young woman and I was rude to her. I felt touchy, on edge, and know that I was stubborn and nasty to everyone. Dad came to see us on Boxing Day and I was moody and spiteful, but when he left I cried.

Margaret was a tragic figure after her mother went away. 'The grown-ups didn't seem to realize how much I was hurting inside: I've been fifteen years in this family and now mum has spoiled it all overnight.'

A fifteen-year-old boy expressed the helplessness so many such children feel:

> They asked me who I wanted to live with. It's like being asked if you want to cut off your arm or your leg. Someone has to get

> hurt. I don't want to hurt dad, he's been hurt enough—but how can I turn my back on mum?

I asked the young people if they felt such group meetings were helpful. Most of them said they were, 'especially after the first one'. They found that sharing experiences was better than struggling on alone. But one boy of fourteen said: 'Yes, we all find comfort in a way, but coming here makes me feel sort of *un*special.' Then he added, thoughtfully, 'I suppose it shows how confused I am.'

Confusion, which so often leads to depression, is usually the result of the lack of information, indefinite plans for the future, uncertain or unreliable arrangements for contact visits, and unanswered questions (see Chapter 2). At this stage, clearcut times and places for meeting the parent they do not live with are essential. Later, when life has settled down, these will hopefully become more flexible. Trust and willingness on every side is vital: rigid timetables must be set up and adhered to. This will start to recreate some of the lost security.

Discipline

A parent feeling guilty, or uncertain of their children's feelings—especially if she is still fearful of losing them—may over-indulge them. In return, the children will test her to the limit. Such infuriating behaviour occurs in all families, and it is difficult to assess how much is due to their loss. In most cases, it is caused by feelings of insecurity—the children are *willing* a parent to discipline them.

When they visit the parent who seldom sees them, there is likely to be more spoiling. A child therapist recognizes this is a familiar problem and advises: 'Do things *with* the kids, not *for* them.'

Sometimes competition between parents gives rise to exploitation. Even at twelve years old, Colin saw what his parents were up to: 'Dad gave me a leather jacket last week, so the next day mum bought me some leather trainers. I was chuffed. Then dad took me to a five-star hotel and mum took me to a theatre. I knew she couldn't afford it, and anyway I'd rather have gone to football. How can I stop them? They don't have to *buy* my love.'

Other children often play one parent against another—not unknown in families living together—but in separated families this can cause much bitterness and recrimination ('Dad lets me stay out until ten o'clock'; 'Mum lets us watch late-night movies'). The ideal answer is for parents to agree on basic rules for both homes. Sometimes an experienced mediator, or a wise grandmother can be useful here.

A father longing to be with his children far more often than the suggested Sunday afternoon must try to accept that for the moment he must just collect and return the children on time, and promise to be at the appointed place the following week.

Difficult relationships

The responsibilities of parenthood may become more challenging after divorce. Marital breakdown is associated with heightened levels of all forms of child neglect and abuse—not only from fathers. One mother, following a bitter relationship with her husband, could never form a healthy rapport with her six-year-old son. 'He's as stupid as his dad,' she would say, and they began to provoke each other.

Someone to talk to

After a while, children usually find the parent they live with the person they will confide in, although for some this never happens. On the whole, girls talk with their friends, while boys—if they talk at all—will confide in siblings, or girlfriends.

Taken into care

When care does what it says—cares—then a brief time of care (by a local authority) for a child who would otherwise be with an overstressed mother or father can be a salvation. The parent has time to relax, find work and/or a new home, and so long as parental visits are kept up, the outcome can be beneficial. Often *shared care* is entered into, when a children's home or a foster parent will share the care of children if a parent requests help. All parents left alone should consider this alternative as a temporary measure when events seem too overwhelming. This alleviates any fears they may have about not being able to get their child *out* of care when they have found a settled home.

Working out the best arrangements

Living with one parent and visiting the other *can* be a happy arrangement. There is no tension, no jealousy, just a natural 'popping round' when they feel like it. These are the sort of situations we don't often hear about, but they do exist.

'It really runs smoothly,' says Jill, fifteen. 'It's better than the old home with all that arguing. We hardly ever saw dad, and mum was always in a temper, or crying. Now they're both good company, and I know they both love us.'

There are no rigid recipes for success—there are no two identical families. Each has to work out the best solution within their own situation:

(1) A couple were in full agreement that their three children stay in the marital home with their mother. Soon there were problems with Jack, the eldest boy. He disobeyed his mother and refused to see his father. Finally, he admitted he was afraid to see his father as he felt he might want to stay with him. Sensibly, his mother asked him: 'Why don't you live with dad?' Since then, it has been a great success. Jack visits his mother, brother and sister whenever he wants to.

(2) Deirdre is only five and spends alternate weeks with her father and mother—against all the professional theories of parenting—but it seems to work well. She is a happy child, very loving and natural with both her parents. They live in the same town, Deirdre has no heartbreaking goodbyes each week, and she loves both her homes.

(3) For one family, life was too hard after dad left—he was violent, impossible even on day visits—yet the two children were upset at the thought of never seeing him. A counsellor suggested that he write to them and now they have started a correspondence. They all enjoy this contact, plus the occasional phone call, and feel 'Dad is still part of the family'.

A death in the family

Elizabeth and Alan lived with their father—they were twelve and thirteen when he died suddenly. Though they went to live with their mother who welcomed them with open arms, they both felt she had never wanted them. 'She never even challenged dad's application for us to live with him.' Actually, their mother desperately wanted them, but knew that she had less to offer them than their father. The children still feel *unwanted*, and their mother feels a *guilt* that she only has them living with her because of their father's death.

Sandra, at fourteen, lived with her mother after her father deserted them. Her mother died of cancer, so her father came to fetch her. Sandra sensed at once how reluctant he was. She realized then that he had never wanted her, and she was filled with anger and refused to live with him. Finally, she was allowed to go to a foster parent.

A death can increase the bitterness in a separated family. June and Alison were living with their mother when they heard of their father's death in Scotland. To their mother's horror, they accused her of 'letting dad die'. 'If you hadn't turned him out he'd be alive today!'

Appointing a guardian

If one parent has lost contact with the children, the parent they live with will probably want to make provisions in his/her will appointing a guardian in the event of his/her death. The children may wish to help choose a favourite relative or god-parent; this sometimes helps to alleviate a child's very natural fear of losing *both* parents. However, this is not a straightforward process, and legal advice should always be sought.

The marital home

Where possible, it is always better for the children if the marital home is *not* sold. If they can stay there with whichever parent it is arranged they are to live with, they will at least have one stability in the background. However, if the 'absent' parent is forced to live in a far inferior home, the situation could be uncomfortable for the children: father may be in a bed-sit while still paying a mortgage on the family house; mother may have chosen to leave and be in a one-room flat, or living with her parents.

Conversely, if the 'absent' parent, usually the father, retains the marital home while mother and children move away, this can also work well. The children's visits will then be on home ground, with no need for constant outings.

Still belonging to both parents

A welfare officer summed up his experiences of families living in two homes: 'If your children develop a feeling of belonging—really being part of—two parents, even when they live miles apart, then you can rest assured your divorce has had the best possible outcome.'

6

School: A Hurdle or a Haven?

About two-thirds of all children from divorced homes show marked changes in their school behaviour. Work suffers from lack of concentration and daydreaming; behaviour becomes aggressive or rudely antisocial. This in turn spoils children's friendships, making them feel very isolated, in spite of the high instance of one-parent families. (The proportion, in British schools, is one in eight or one in three in some inner city areas.)

Many children suffer the practical problems brought on by parents fighting at night, making it impossible to do homework; others may be having a change of home, perhaps several changes, going to foster homes or being moved back and forth between parents—all very unsettling situations. Others may be emotionally drained after long-drawn-out arguments and indecisions. All will be suffering shock from their changed circumstances: 'It's happened to me, why me?' Suddenly money is tight, they cannot afford school dinners, or go to the cinema, or buy videos.

How can schools help?

Schools have an important role in helping children cope with problems caused by separation and divorce. First, a school can no longer assume a pupil's family to be the traditional two (natural)-parent home. The word *family* may cover a wide variety of human interrelationships: separated parents, step-parents, foster mothers, twice-divorced parents, unmarried mothers. These relationships do not necessarily fail to provide a secure, or happy, home; continual conflict and/or constant changes are the more usual causes of a child's distress and disturbed behaviour.

The head of a junior mixed school said: 'Father often moves over the road to another family on the housing estate. You never know who is married to whom. This is why many teachers feel it best for children to look on school as a secure haven, where they can forget home disturbances—it's five hours of peace for a child.'

To provide any of the practical help needed, the school must be informed of a pupil's basic living arrangements: who the child lives with; the mother's surname, if different from that of her child; contact arrangements with the other parent.

Even though a child is living with one parent, in *most* family situations, since the Children Act, *both* parents with responsibility have the right to be involved in schooling. Both can be consulted on major decisions, such as exams, change of school, medical matters, etc. Unless there is a court injunction denying contact with one parent, a school will remain impartial and encourage both parents to get copies of termly reports and attend Parents' Evenings.

There can be a wide variety of circumstances following a divorce or separation, and many local Education Authorities are setting up telephone helplines to assist schools in ensuring that they only contact those legally entitled to be consulted on matters/decisions concerning each child.

At worst, school is a place where a parent will try to abduct a child illegally. We saw (in Chapter 4) how children often do not see the 'snatching' as the frightening experience adults imagine, but it is a big responsibility for schools to be drawn into these legal and emotional matters.

Accurate information is needed if a parent is denied legal access, when a school is *not* allowed to show or send him/her any material relating to that child. The National Council for One-Parent Families provides helpful guidelines for parents, pupils and teachers:

> A school can restrict access to a child if it feels the child to be at risk or in distress from the parental conflict. In effect, a school could act *in loco parentis*—acting in a way that it considers a reasonable parent would.
>
> By the same token, a school could allow a child to see an

> estranged parent against the wishes of the other, provided the child had expressly and repeatedly stated a wish to do so and *there was no legal bar on it.*

Schools are in the most advantageous position to acknowledge, assess and provide support for children from disrupted homes. The routine of school, the familiar discipline, the mixing with his own peer group, the very *ordinariness* and hustle of each school day, is comforting to a child whose home is far from comfortable or ordinary. However, it depends on head teachers whether their school's policy is to assume the responsibility of including counselling care within their curriculum.

A high proportion of teachers are divorced parents, which means they often prefer a school where the home lives of pupils are not referred to—their own emotions being too near the surface for objective discussion.

Other teachers are aware of the impossibility of separating a child's social, personal and academic education. Major changes such as a death, divorce, change of home or carer must affect a child's learning abilities and as such have to be made known to their teachers.

LEA's should be able to provide guidelines for schools. But there is little doubt that all schools do prefer to be told *by* the parents of any major changes in a pupil's life. If a teacher hears of such changes from outside, or even from the child concerned, he will not feel free to discuss the subject—the parent might not wish that.

Advice to parents

The head teacher of a large London school has found that some parents do not inform the school when they divorce because it does not occur to them that their separation will have any impact on their child's schooling, now or later:

> Once parents do let us know, the ethos in this school is such that the appropriate staff are informed, and will be alert for

> any signs of unusual or prolonged stress in the child. We also confirm which parent the child is living with, and ensure that she/he knows where to turn for help if needed—perhaps to our educational psychologist. We do not claim to be able to lessen the damage done to children through traumas at home—but we are in the best possible position from which to give them at least some of the support they will need in order to mature socially as well as academically.

Sadly, not all teachers are as discerning, or compassionate; also, parents frequently decide that to suggest their child be treated differently in any way would be harmful to them. The mother of nine-year-old twins was heard to say: 'I don't think teachers should pry into their pupils' lives, it's not their business.'

Nursery and play school

A sensitive nursery teacher will recognize when a tiny child's reluctance to leave a parent each morning is something more than normal, and tears do not change to laughter in minutes after the parent has left:

> Usually, this is a child who has suffered the loss of a parent—and the teacher can support the single parent here. Perhaps dad has gone away and mother is having to go to work. She feels guilty and the child senses this uncertainty. A wise teacher can provide a clock, or a toy watch, to give the child a solid sense of time, learning that when the hands point to 3 o'clock, or an alarm rings, mummy *will* return. Towards that time, he may begin to tremble or cry, but soon he will learn to trust grown-ups again.

Primary school

In primary and infant schools, teachers like to develop friendly relationships with a family, and if they are kept in ignorance of changes in the home situation they can be unwittingly insensitive to the children (Isn't daddy going to fetch you today?). A teacher has been left not knowing whom to hand a child to at the end of the afternoon. They like to know the circumstances so that, for example, making cards for Mother's or Father's Day will not embarrass a child with no father, or two mothers. A teacher must never say to her class: 'Get your parents to sign this.' She must say: 'Get your mum or dad to sign this, whoever is at home tonight.'

Many children refuse to tell the school, and make up stories if asked why they are not concentrating on their work. Children never want to be made a fuss of—they just want someone to *know*. School is often a relief: 'It's still the same, but my home has changed now mum has gone. I like my school, I don't want pity.'

At a typical inner-city school, where the catchment area is multiracial, and 50 per cent of the parents are unemployed, there is at least a 20 per cent absence of fathers. The head has appointed a special teacher to work with these families, and in many similar schools a post of *home-school liaison teacher* has been created. Chaotic discipline at home—often including incidences of juvenile crime, vandalism and physical violence, can soon be guessed at by teachers; they will take note of irritability, lack of concentration, isolation, aggression, unhappiness—all of which can be the result of a parent leaving home.

Maybe things were not so good *before* the parent left home, but in most cases real stress shows in a child when the 'single' parent has lost control. Poverty plays a large part in the lowering of living standards: mother is struggling to make ends meet; father may be breaking the carefully planned arrangements for contact, or have disappeared; teenagers are becoming violent; tempers fray, the children run wild and play truant from school.

Stepchildren

School can be a secure place for a confused child of stepparents. A good teacher will notice if a child is disturbed by other children asking her about the new family, new name. Some children change their names just for school to prevent teasing and confusion, using their *real* father's name at home. Some children, of course, lap up all the attention, show off, while others hate it and become embarrassed. Some of them pretend their stepparent is their real father, just to be 'the same as everyone else'.

Teachers can help such children by making their school day as calm and ordered as possible—watching for signs of prolonged anxiety, when they should never hesitate to call in further help. Mothers often do not like to ask for help, seeing this as a sign of failure, but if a teacher suggests a meeting, perhaps with the school psychologist, then it can be seen as a move to help the child, rather than the mother.

When a teacher asked tactfully if one family could make an effort to come to the art exhibition, the stepfather said: 'He's got everything he wants, I gave him a new paintbox.' Asked if she could get off work to attend, the mother said: 'I do my job, you do yours.'

Finally, that child became aggressive, broke a plate over another child's head, spilt painting water over his own drawings. The head had to call both parents to the school, whereupon the boy was delighted. Even in the head's study, the parents argued—father telling mother she was a bad parent; mother saying father spoiled the child on his infrequent visits. They agreed to see a family therapist, and the boy became easier—I suspect only because of more attention—he felt his parents were at last acknowledging his existence. It was definitely *not* due to mother and father agreeing to be better parents.

Going to a new school

If a child is new to the school, owing to a separation which involved a family move, then extra attention must be given—the child's sense of isolation will be acute, and if she can be allowed to talk of her old school, old friends, her family, her pets, she will be helped to feel less strange. A thoughtless, 'We don't do that in *this* school,' can only add to a child's desperate loneliness.

School refusal

This is a classic problem, and can have many causes. Following divorce, the usual cause is fear—one parent has deserted them, and they dread that the other will also disappear while they are away. As going-home time approaches, they can be filled with feelings of panic. Only constant assurances that mother *is* coming back, and that teacher will be with her until then, will eventually allow a child to relax—but it may take many weeks or even months.

'Teacher is my friend'

At this age level, children are likely to spend most of each day with one teacher—so that the relationship between them can resemble that of a surrogate mother. Such rapport is obviously comforting for a child from a disturbed home—he may not necessarily tell his teacher all his worries, but he will certainly feel free to do so if he wishes.

Sally, aged seven, a bright child, suddenly began to talk 'baby talk' and to scribble instead of writing in her workbooks; at lunchtime she would ask for a spoon and demand to be fed. Her teacher wisely made no comments, and arranged a meeting with Sally's mother and father, the school head and a family therapist. Her mother did most of the talking, explaining that Sally had become seriously ill, 'almost mentally unbalanced', and would throw tantrums every night, screaming and throwing herself on the floor. 'I have to put her head under the cold shower before she will stop.'

They found that the parents were about to separate, that every evening they had violent fights—and Sally's screaming was a vain attempt to drown the sounds. At school, she was trying to recall her babyhood, when there were no fights and she was happy. Eventually, it was arranged that the little girl live with her father, and a kindly aunt came to housekeep for them both. In a matter of months Sally was a model pupil again—reading and writing well above average for her age.

Physical signs of distress

Pressures on children may be reflected in their health. Some get sore throats, stomach cramps, earache, headache and skin rashes. Asthma may worsen, an outward expression of a child's attempt to deal with emotional problems. A school nurse must always be told of a child's home situation.

Emotional deprivation

A child psychiatrist points out that: 'In the affluent classes, emotional deprivation is rarely suspected or detected,' and here again assumptions are readily made. In many small schools in 'privileged' areas, a child's feelings of sadness and rejection can be heartbreaking. 'I was a mistake,' said Charles, aged nine. It took an understanding teacher many hours of patient confidence-boosting that term to allow the young boy to feel wanted.

Vanessa refused to eat her school dinners, and her teacher spoke with the au pair girl who fetched the eight-year-old from school. 'Her mother says she is showing off and not to take any notice.' As time went on the child became more antisocial and the head teacher made more enquiries. The mother had turned her husband out of the house 'because he is never here'. Following the divorce, she took a job which involved travelling—leaving Vanessa in the care of a succession of young girls. The father was living in a London hotel where Vanessa would spend every other weekend. Her only friends were two sons of other wealthy, divorced parents, whose sole amusement was to spend hours sliding down the laundry shoot in the five-star hotel.

Sadly, neither parent ever fully understood why their daughter was showing off—it was the only way she knew to get a little attention, and perhaps love.

Aged six, Robert came to me during breaktime and said: 'Grown-ups can't help falling in love.' His face was all innocence as he continued: 'My mummy was walking in the park and she met Peter and fell in love with him. It wasn't her fault,' he said, rather fiercely, as if he had been told not to forget his lines. It was touching—I was sure his young mother was trying to introduce him gradually to her separation. 'We're going to live in a new house,' he added. Would he mention his daddy? Should I? 'Daddy is going to stay in our old house so I can visit him.' This was easier for me. 'Good, then you can come and see me and your friends at school. You will have *two* lovely homes to go to, that's exciting, Robert.' When she fetched him I told his mother that Robert had hinted at her new plans. She looked relieved, saying she had meant to tell me later that week.

I then realized that, however articulate his parents, however thoughtful, loving and concerned they are—a child is going to need someone else to turn to. Not necessarily to intrude, nothing can change the situation, nothing can alter his parents' decision, nothing must be criticized—that is not what a child wants. But he *does* want someone to listen. Saying it aloud, getting it off his chest, helped Robert to share his anxiety over what was happening to his family.

I have heard teachers say: 'We don't want to know about things like that, not at school, keep that sort of thing for your home.' For those children, it is far more cruel than the teachers realize, for there may be *no one else* to talk to.

So how can teachers help?

Jennifer, aged ten, began to have behaviour problems in school, showing defiance to authority. She was very irritable, fighting with other children, coming to class with dirty hands and unbrushed hair. Her mother was impatient with her because she knew Jennifer wanted to live with her father. 'Not until you are sixteen and know your own mind.' 'I know it now,' the child replied. She was close to her father, whom she saw every fortnight. When her mother went to a parents' evening, Jennifer's wise teacher said: 'The best way to keep children is sometimes to let them go.' Expecting to discuss her daughter's poor school work, the mother was upset; but after further discussion with the teacher, then with the head, the educational psychologist and a social worker, she arranged to speak to her ex-husband. Finally they all agreed it would be better for Jennifer to live with her father. 'I love mummy so much for letting me do that,' said the child, who still sees her mother a lot. Her school work and behaviour improved within days.

Jennifer's teacher was able to provide unique support for the whole family, but many primary teachers need guidelines before they can offer help to parents:

(1) Be available as trusted confidantes—never *pressurizing* children to talk.
(2) Keep close contact with the parent the child lives with, comparing any changes in a child's behaviour or work; show a parent that her child's problems are not unique and *will* lessen.
(3) Help parents to appreciate that adults and children have different perspectives on relationships—that their child is not necessarily feeling the same emotions as they are.
(4) Continue to treat these children exactly the same as the others in class, creating a stable, familiar atmosphere.

It is sometimes difficult for a teacher to remain impartial when two parents come with opposing stories. They have to remember that it is the children who suffer.

Two six-year-old girls, who were great friends, became stepsisters when one's father married the other's mother following the two divorces. I heard them arguing over who had *stolen* the other parent. It was painful to listen to them in class and hear a note of adult cynicism creeping in. Many of the words they used were obviously repeated from their parents, and I sensed the bitterness of the home atmosphere they must both be living in. Even with the special teacher's help, and the cooperation of the parents, it still required a great deal of sympathy, of listening, and of explaining that the two parents had *chosen* to marry, that neither one had been a thief!

Secondary school

In a large school, where pupils move from classroom to classroom for each lesson with different teachers for each subject, there is seldom a chance to form the sort of personal rapport with a child that can be achieved in a junior school.

In some schools, the children are not aware which teachers are available if needed. This is left to individual members of staff, and there is no denying some are more able at counselling work than others. Teachers, by definition, are there to teach, and a child may feel she does not want to be *taught*, but simply to be understood. Her parents are telling her what to do, where to live, who to live with. She wants someone who will hear *her* opinion, *her* anxieties for the future.

Christine put her trust in her art teacher and found herself pouring out all about her mother running off with another man and how angry her father was:

> I thought she would be sympathetic. Instead she started telling me what to do—things like understanding mum, how women need to express themselves and how dad would learn from looking after me. Nothing about *me*, or *my* feelings. I wished I had kept quiet.

An exchange of views with senior pupils is good—but at times of stress it is the person who listens with her heart who will be able to support an adolescent. In some schools, a school counsellor visits once a week, with whom pupils can arrange private talks. Erica, sixteen, said: 'I was shy for my teacher to know all my feelings—but with the Counsellor I could let it all out—it felt good.'

What teachers must watch out for

Signs of stress are not always obvious. The common elements such as lack of concentration and a decline in academic standard can be due to causes other than the break-up of a home. However, when these are accompanied by depression, possible aggressive responses to criticism, and sudden defiance of all authority, a sensitive teacher would do well to make herself available for discussion and also talk with that child's friends to enlist their understanding. Some schools have a special quiet room for such talks.

A few children become *more* attentive at school, producing excellent work, so that their teacher feels they are coping well. But their industry may be their way of coping with difficulties at home, and the school must be watchful for any signs of a belated reaction or breakdown.

Boys around fourteen are particularly prone to depression and play truant from school a lot more than girls as a result of their parents' divorce. Much of this male aggression in adolescence is attributable to a deep resentment and anger against fathers, and so against all authority, for denying them a model of true masculinity. They feel deprived, and do not know how to handle gentleness or sensitivity. They tend to compensate for that by violent and abusive behaviour. Male teachers who can help these youngsters to cultivate the gentle, nurturing sides of their natures will be performing a service vital to that child and to his family.

Parents can help too

Many parents, understandably, will be so wrapped up in their own worries during this stressful time that they look on school as a place to rid themselves of their children for six or seven hours a day. Many are working, and under great pressure. A parent may come in and talk about herself, pour out her resentment of her ex-partner and use the school as her counsellor; she often has to have it pointed out that her child does *not* carry the same resentment against his father, and would like to feel free to see him as before. Another parent may come in and say that her children are 'doing fine', when in fact their work or behaviour at school tells a different story.

The basic rule for parents is that the child's feelings should be paramount. Sometimes, it is a teacher who will explain to a parent what those feelings are, and surprise a parent with the children's wishes—usually the opposite of what the parent has *assumed* them to be.

June's mother told her teacher that 'Her life will soon be stable. I am remarrying and we will be able to give her a happy home.' Later that day, June said to her teacher: 'If mum marries that guy, I'll leave home.'

Role of the school

Some schools issue a report card which the child has to have signed by the head, so that the parent the child lives with, the child, and the head have an agreement as to what is reasonable behaviour. Sometimes a special bedtime is laid down, and in worse cases a child may be under oath not to hit his mother, or steal, hurt his sister, kick the dog, or play truant.

No teacher can suddenly turn an aggressive child into an angel, or a disinterested and dispirited parent into a model mother or father—but if a child sees that a teacher cares enough about him to spend time with him and to enlist the parent's help, he will appreciate that attention. 'No one ever asked *my* opinion before,' commented Brian, aged thirteen, who suggested a similar programme for his younger brother.

Attitudes of children and teachers

'We're one-parent kids, we suffer.' 'I'm from a broken home, I'm going to be a delinquent, so what?'

This happens—children need support and sympathy—and it will not take an A-stream intelligence to find out how to get it!

Conversely, many teachers show this attitude themselves: 'He's from a broken home, let's put him in the lower grade.' They anticipate trouble, whereas in many cases such children, *because* of their traumatic home lives, have become more mature, more compassionate young people, and with praise and encouragement from teachers, could be an asset to their schools.

At fourteen Susan said: 'I can get away with a lot at school. All my teachers assume I will be a problem so they are never cross with me. They know mum ran away so they think I'm unstable. In fact, dad is doing very well in his job, and is a great parent, coping well with us all. It has kind of brought us closer. But the teachers still treat me as a deprived child.'

Teachers tend to forget, also, that a great many *two*-parent homes are not at all conducive to work and concentration either.

Other teachers point out that: 'There is less fighting at home when the parents live apart, so the children are quieter; they are getting *more* attention from both parents, and there are few arguments over discipline.' One head added his advice: 'Never write children off because their parents have split up; you can help them transcend the situation.'

Pastoral care

Secondary schools have comprehensive pastoral care systems set up to make sure that the general welfare of children is looked after as thoroughly as the educational aspects. No taboos remain on subject matter; what does matter is the *approach* to each subject. Helping teenagers to form attitudes is a huge responsibility—although teachers are generally better equipped in their knowledge of a child's various stages of development than parents, and appreciate which subjects (alcohol and drug abuse, sexual perversion, bereavement counselling, etc.) are appropriate for each class. Moral education is not teaching what is right and what is wrong; it means helping each person to recognize that moral choices exist.

An experienced conciliator feels this 'pastoral' care and advice could be extended even further to include:

> Teaching children how to empathize and relate to others. A fourth R, *relationship*, could be added to the three Rs which are now called *basic skills*. Knowing how to relate is as important in life as being literate and numerate.

He also suggests that:

> Teaching our children how to react to conflict without running away from it or resorting to violence should be a basic part of the school curriculum. Learning how to listen and respond to other people with whom you disagree, that is, how to negotiate, should be a priority in education which could lead to more satisfactory relationships generally.

School leavers

Amongst the advice given to sixth-formers, I would stress the need for constructive warnings on leaving home. Most teenagers want to show their independence as soon as possible, and those in divided families tend to be even more anxious to leave home. No one wants to dampen their enthusiasm, their sense of adventure, but they must be armed with practical information on what to expect in the world 'out there', especially if they come from country areas. They may think they know it all—but listen to Pete, eighteen, on this experience:

> I would warn any school leaver that *all* the odds are against him finding work or accommodation in a big city—anywhere in the world. I left home to get away from my stepfather and had to sleep rough for three months. What hope did I have of looking respectable enough for a job interview after a night on a park bench?

Boarding school

Parents have been known to send their children to boarding school while divorce proceedings are going on. 'It will be better for them to be right away from the drama.' But unless this has been arranged and discussed long before any family troubles began, a child will feel doubly rejected if he is suddenly sent away from home.

Kate was ten, and very difficult at her junior school. 'Boarding school would be good for her,' advised the headmistress. Halfway through her first term, Kate was caught stealing things from other children. 'I felt so cut off from all the worrying changes that were happening at home, so I *tried* to get expelled.'

At least Kate knew about her parents' divorce. Barbara, at twelve, was sent away 'for your health, dear'. One night in her dormitory, another girl said, 'Your parents are separated, aren't they? I expect that's why you're here! That means they will be getting a divorce soon.' Barbara had no idea of this, and wept bitterly to think the other girls knew before she had been told.

Polly, aged fourteen, was difficult at home, playing one parent against another with outrageous spite, and the child psychiatrist advised them to send her to boarding school. 'You must tell her that you are sending her away because it will give you a chance to get on and end your unhappy marriage. You must lead your own lives and show your daughter the way to lead hers.'

To their surprise it worked. Polly began to show independence and spent alternate holidays with each parent.

Much depends on the teachers concerned. One teenager said that her boarding school was: 'Very nice, but the teachers picked out all the girls from divided homes to give extra treats to; we felt horribly conspicuous.'

Not easy to get it just right, is it! Boarding school teachers are in a unique position to listen for hidden questions, uncover buried fears, clarify misconceptions. There will be times when it will be appropriate to leave children alone. They need privacy; adults tend to confuse privacy with independence.

Many parents feel it more caring to wait until their children leave school before they separate. Their motives are compassionate, and if they can avoid too much tension in the household, it must often be a worthwhile sacrifice for their children. However, they sometimes forget that teenagers who are about to leave home for the first time, if they know that home is about to be disbanded, start their adult lives with a terrible feeling of insecurity. This often affects their university studies, or their first months as an apprentice, very seriously.

7
Stepchildren: Yours, Mine and Ours

'I knew I was different when I told my friend I was spending Christmas with my stepmother's ex-husband's mother.'

The complexities of stepfamilies were brought home to me by a girl recalling her childhood memories, which for her had begun at the age of five. 'I have never known a normal home atmosphere, have never actually lived with a couple who love each other.'

It seems to me that becoming a stepfamily can have more significant and far-reaching effects on children than their parents' divorce. Neither the myth of the wicked stepmother, nor the getting together of two households to make one big 'Happy Family', describe the harsh reality of being a stepchild for most children. I feel the very term stepmother or stepfather is unfortunate. In a few exceptional cases where the children are babies and one natural parent has died or disappeared, then a replacement parent can be acceptable. Otherwise, it is adding salt to their wounds to suggest a child who has been forced to live apart from one parent should look on another adult as a mother or father.

'Of course, I could never replace your mother,' said one newlywed to two sisters of eight and ten. 'Well, nobody asked you to, did they?' she heard in reply. Where the relationship is harmonious, I have heard the term *extra* mother being used—surely more accurate, and less threatening.

First reactions

Divorce usually takes place around the tenth year of marriage, so the partners and their children are still young. These parents want to be given a second chance, and to make better homes for their children—so the number of remarriages grows each year.

'Will you be our daddy?' is not an unusual request for a four-year-old to make to any male who comes into the house! To be a two-parent family again is what most of them want. The reality, however, is not always so simple: 'Go away, you're *not* my daddy!' requires tactful handling—preschool children can amaze parents with their sharp perceptions.

For the older children, there is more conflict. 'Who is this young woman who dad keeps bringing home?' 'Is she going to bring those weepy children with her?' 'We've got a mum, thank you, we don't need you.'

If parents think separation is hard to explain, then remarrying is even harder, with far fewer agencies to seek help from. *Any hope of your parents getting together again is shattered*. Children's reactions to this realization are varied but forceful.

Tom began to mess up the house, deliberately emptying drawers and cupboards, and unmaking the beds. His brother Bill was quieter, 'almost as though something inside him had died'. Both boys realized their mother was *not* coming home—they were finally mourning their loss.

Natalie's mother began to criticize her father, tried to stop the child visiting him, insinuating gossip about his affairs, grumbling at his failure to send them money. In the same breath, she said she was marrying a new husband. 'You must be nice to him.' Natalie resented this stranger, and when he prevented her phoning her father, she was frantic:

> I was thirteen and felt I had a right to talk to my own father. When dad moved house, I didn't tell mum his new phone number.

How sad when children have to resort to underhand ways of contacting an absent parent. Carla (nine) and Mike (eleven) had a prearranged phone signal of three rings to their father. They lived with their mother and stepfather:

> When mum got pregnant she said she didn't want me any more. Mike stuck up for me, so my stepfather said he must leave too. We crept out that night and phoned dad—he picked us up and we've never been back.

Plunged into a strange household

We all remember visiting our friends' homes when young—yet even if we liked them, it was always good to come home. 'Jane's father makes her do her homework on Saturday mornings.' 'Pam's family don't have meals in the kitchen!'

Other people's houses are different. So imagine if you, as a child, were expected to *live* in one, permanently.

It is asking a lot of any child, perhaps still trying desperately to cope with a parent who has left her, to move into a strange man's home. She has to watch him take over her mother's life, feel him intruding upon the time she feels *she* needs with her mother. Even if her own father was never a good parent, it is still going to bring on a range of powerful emotions—fear, resentment, anger and often great sorrow—a helpless feeling that life is crashing on around her and there's nothing she can do to stop it or, preferably, to turn it back.

Celia, aged eleven: 'How can I feel happy in this house? These people are not *family*. I feel like a guest, yet I can't go home.'

Hasty remarriage

A stepfamily is a family born of loss—either through death or divorce. Either loss needs a time of mourning—which according to many family therapists may take from three to five years. If children are plunged too soon into a new family, they will not be ready emotionally to take on added anxieties: 'Will this mean I never see daddy?' 'How will I fit in with these other children?' This is when there are accusations of 'stealing' a parent.

At nine, Annie loved her mother dearly, but said: 'I did my damnedest to wreck her wedding.' When the champagne was opened, she refused to drink a toast. 'What is there to celebrate?' she asked loudly.

The wedding can be a controversial issue in itself. Nigel (thirteen): 'I asked dad why he didn't invite me to his wedding, and he said his wife and stepchildren didn't want him to. That hurt a lot. I knew then I didn't come first with dad any more.'

When a widowed parent remarries, everyone smiles sympathetically on the children who, when very young, are often included in the wording of the marriage service. But when it is a divorced parent the child is seldom considered. 'The guests didn't even shake my hand afterwards' (Gerry, aged fourteen). They really do need a lot of attention and be made to feel they are included.

Others feel they cannot face the occasion. Martin phoned his father on the morning of his mother's wedding. 'Mum is getting married today and I don't like Bill. May I come back to you?' Martin was lucky in that his father had the intelligence, and courage, to speak to his ex-wife, even at this awkward time; they agreed to let the child stay with his father for a few weeks, and then to have far more flexible visiting times.

Some parents, especially fathers, never tell their children until *after* they have married again. Craig, at twelve, received a letter from his father telling him the news, although he sees him every day. 'Remember you met Marilyn last month? Well, she's my new wife.' The boy's mother was left to cope with his confused questions.

When mother remarries

> I've lived with mum for four years since dad left. Now she's married Jim and though he's quite nice, mum and me never do things together any more. She goes with him to the cinema without me. She puts TV programmes on that *he* wants, and cooks dinners *he* likes.

Rosie was jealous. But what of Rachel, who had two stepbrothers as well as a stepfather to live with. The boys' mother was dead, and used this to taunt Rachel. 'It's all right for you, you can go to your dad when you like, but we can't ever get to see our mum.' 'That's it, I've *got* a dad, so I don't want yours!' the little girl shouted back.

All under ten, those children already had a grasp of the main issue involved: the undeniable fact that parents are *for ever*; there are no ex-parents, only ex-husbands and ex-wives.

Obviously, the attitude of the stepfather will help the children, though his role is far from easy, especially if he moves into the mother's home. 'Who said you could sit in dad's place?' 'Dad never puts his slippers on in the sitting-room.'

It is a difficult act to perform well, and boys from nine to fifteen are known to be least willing to accept a stepfather. Barry, who left home at sixteen, says: 'I wish my stepdad had been less easygoing. We had no discipline, it was chaos.'

Ken had the opposite experience, but also left home as soon as possible. 'My stepfather was frightening, he was so strict. I hated him, he never even let me mention dad in front of mum.'

The natural mother might also have been a poor parent, putting all the blame on her ex-husband, tearing their children apart with her harsh criticisms of their father. Neil (fourteen):

> Mum thought it would be lovely for me to have a father-figure always there, as dad lives in America, but I hated this man just because he *was* there—trying to be my father. If I'd met him as a friend he'd be fine, he's a great guy. But I hate his playacting the father role.

It is that tragic inability of so many parents to break away emotionally from the past. When they do manage it, mothers often create a wonderful new marriage. Counsellors stress the benefit to children of witnessing, possibly for the first time, the pattern of a happy relationship, with no friction.

Meanwhile, a father can feel a jealousy bordering on despair when he knows his own child is living with another father-figure. For this reason, many fathers keep away, either through resignation to the loss, or through a genuine feeling that it will be better for the child. The child may feel differently.

Graham is a quiet, intelligent boy of fifteen, who lives with his mother and stepfather. His one sorrow is that his father seldom contacts him. Even when he was about to sit his GCSE exams, his father never phoned or wished him luck. Graham noticed how concerned his stepfather was with *his* sons and saw how a father could be. His stepfather never made him feel left out, but

Graham still wished that his own dad was there. 'I felt ashamed for him, I suppose.'

When father remarries

'Why didn't dad look like that with mum?' A bewildered teenager notices her father's happiness with his new wife and finds it hard to be happy herself. Cathy, twelve:

> I feel dad's wife is more special than me now. I can't get dad to myself any more, and Saturdays together are *out*. She always has to come everywhere. I worry about mum too, she's all alone.

> My parents divorced when I was six. I live with mum and we get on well. When I first went to dad and his new wife at weekends it was horrible. There are two boys and I hated seeing dad being so good to them. I suppose I was jealous. Now I'm older, I enjoy their company, they are all very kind to me. But I never dare tell mum what fun we have.

Again, the lack of communication between the natural parents is causing so much unnecessary distress. Mandy, at twelve, has had a happier experience:

> My stepmother actually got mum to tell her the basic set-up in my own home, so I know that when she tells me to do something it's because my mum wants it—that's OK.

Molly, fourteen, had a stepmother who had no such compassionate ideas: 'I don't think she cared if I was in the house, let alone in bed, each night.'

Two younger children had good cause to think of their stepmother as 'wicked':

> The first week she came into our house everything changed. She sold a lot of our furniture, took down all our pictures,

even in our bedroom. When dad came home in the evenings, he would go off with Sally and we hardly ever saw him.

Part-time stepchildren

Tim's father lives in their old family home, but visiting is still quite an ordeal. 'It's like I'm not family any more.' Tim (nine) clearly loves his father, but his stepsisters resent Tim's weekends with them, and refuse to leave him alone with his dad.

Tim has fairly typical, ambivalent, emotions about it all, saying that he is jealous of his stepsisters having *his* dad as a father, while he has *no* father in his house. On the other hand, when I asked if he would like his mother to marry again, he said, 'No, I know I couldn't cope with that.'

John's stepmother is almost too welcoming when he visits, so that he feels like a guest in his old home. But it is on his return to his mother that his problems start. 'Mum puts me through a sort of quiz every time—she wants to know about dad's family down to the last detail. I don't think dad would like me to tell on him.'

Now he is part of another family, a child's contact with his 'absent' parent becomes even more important. The remarried couple must be seen to give permission willingly for this to continue. Children can accept a stepparent more readily if not required to 'give up' a natural parent to do so.

Stepbrothers and stepsisters

Weekends can be very long when there are two lots of stepchildren around. No one feels really at home, and if lack of communication was part of the problem before, within a stepfamily it can be frightening.

Where possible, families should be introduced long before they are thrown together under one roof—they need warning if they are not going to be the eldest any more, or if they are expected to share rooms, or visit new grandparents.

It usually takes over two years for families to settle down and find a way of living together that suits everyone.

Once they have moved in, however, stepparents have their own problems to sort out; children in divided families can become aware of the fallibility of adults at a very young age. Margaret remembers spending a summer holiday with her father and stepmother:

> There were three children, and my brother and I were determined to hate them—they'd stolen our dad, hadn't they? But when the adults began fighting and seemed to forget about us, we all got together and realized we were in the same boat. That's when I began to see my parents as stupid, instead of dependable.

Margaret's experience is not unusual, and the two lots of children can often become firm friends. 'When I heard my daughter *asking* if she could bring her stepsister with her on a visit, I *knew* things would work out well.' She was right; 'Being *told* to be nice to a stepsister is awful!' said one nine-year-old, but if they make their own friendship they will grow up with a wide-ranging perception of relationships.

Second time around

It does not always stop at one remarriage. Steve has just heard that his stepfather, with whom he has a greater rapport than with his own father, is leaving them. Another man is about to enter their household and Steve is determined *not* to become his friend. 'Not again, I'm tired of being left.'

Some of the children have stories of second and third divorces that almost match the old Hollywood one about the two schoolgirls: 'Digby is a nice stepfather.' 'Yes, I know, we had him last year.'

One girl of fourteen is far more deeply affected: 'When my stepfather divorced my mother I knew then that marriage was an awful thing, nothing but fighting. I would never marry.'

Teenagers

Life as a teenager can be enormous fun, but it is a difficult period—adults suddenly become unsympathetic and life is hard. Life as a stepchild can also be fun, or it can be traumatic. Put the two situations together and adolescent youngsters have a seemingly impossible hurdle to overcome.

Barry found it increasingly hard to face life with his stepmother and her three young children. A sociable boy, he found he spent most of his time with his friends, only coming home occasionally to sleep or eat. His stepmother was hurt, and felt Barry was being rude to her as well as unkind to his father. But this is the boy's way of coping. By seeing very little of his stepfamily, he can enjoy their times together.

Emotional and sexual problems

It is natural that there will be more awareness of sexuality when there are teenagers in the stepfamily. Seeing their mother or father entering into a new relationship may well have aroused great sexual jealousy, anger and often prudery. They will find it extremely difficult to accept a parent's new partner. For girls, having a strange man in the house may be embarrassing, they may feel threatened or frightened. A young boy may well feel resentment against his stepmother, yet at the same time have his early sexual feelings aroused. Emotions become very confused.

In some families, teenage boys and girls will suddenly find themselves in the same home, and this will need careful handling by the adults. Separate rooms are the ideal, and plenty of visitors to the house so that the family relationships are not too claustrophobic.

A baby in the house

A new baby in a stepfamily can be, and usually is, a happy event. It seems the first real *joint* venture they are all undertaking, and it can forge a link that will hopefully keep everyone together.

Other families may find this new arrival just another reason for resentment and jealousy. 'Dad seems to think this baby the most wonderful child in the world—I can't see that it's any better than any of us!' Christopher was only seven, and was perhaps not feeling any more jealous than many children of his age in 'normal' families when a new baby comes on the scene. But once again, great tact will be needed by the parents—extra attention given to the other children, and assurances that they can still have their own bedrooms, toys and precious times alone with mum.

Visiting stepchildren may feel in the way, or less welcome, or even not wanted, if mum is taken up with a new baby—they are denied the excitement a half-brother or sister might bring.

This is one time when the 'other' parent must show the greatest self-discipline and compassion. If he or she can appear to be delighted at the news, the children will feel free to be delighted also. It is hard when they are denied such basic human emotions.

Adopting a stepchild

Some stepchildren want to change their names to that of the stepfather, in order to be 'normal', in other words a family all with the same name. This is not legally possible without the consent of the other natural parent, or the permission of the court.

Janice, aged ten, whose mother wants her new husband to adopt the child, does not want to be adopted and feels her stepfather does not really want this either. 'If I'm adopted, will that mean my stepfather is my *real* father?' she asked the family therapist, who was able to assure her that she and her father could make the decision. 'But I still feel afraid,' she says.

Even when consent is given, the future must be considered. Suppose there is a second divorce? Julian remembers being happy with his mother's new name, but when he grew up and married, he felt, 'I want to be myself.' Only then did he discover that adoption meant *complete* loss of all his rights, inheritance, and connection with his natural father, and with his father's family.

Discipline

This is a difficult subject in a stepfamily's house and one that is frequently mentioned. Ideally, if the two families can get together and talk, it helps to sort out problems of meal and bedtimes, contact visits, likes and dislikes, house rules, etc.

Samantha is a normal, mischievous little girl of five, living with her father and stepmother. Once a month, she spends a long weekend with her mother and stepfather, where she leads a grown-up life: staying up late, going out to eat, using (often strong) adult language.

It takes her patient father several days to calm the little girl down after each visit. He has tried to get the other household to agree on discipline, but they do not want to know. When the two stepfamilies are willing to liaise, it is not necessary to alter their individual lifestyles, but if they can agree on the basic manners and morals they approve of, then the children feel far less bewildered:

> I took my dog up to my room and let him sleep on my bed and my stepmother shouted at me and told me to wash the sheets, and dad heard and they started to fight. I felt it was all my fault, and thought there would be another divorce in our family.

Sadly, these small differences in domestic behaviour do cause separations. It requires that fourth R, relationships, to come into play in such situations.

A child should be told, as far as possible, what is and is not allowed in each house—if one adult has a horror of hamsters or a dislike of dogs that must be respected. Neither household is right, nor wrong, simply different.

No one can avoid all conflicts; the best families in the world have those—misunderstandings arise daily. But within stepfamilies it is well worth the extra effort of explaining the ground rules from the beginning.

Children can be very difficult themselves:

> I see now how much I must have hurt my stepmother. She never wanted me to call her mother, just Gillian. She was loving, and I must have been a pain in the neck. I kept on talking about my own mother, how she baked better cakes, bought better clothes, even drove the car better—not much of which was true. Gillian was very patient. But looking back, I was determined to hate her.

Such situations can cause quarrels and real unhappiness between a married couple. It is not just childish naughtiness, it is a very real, human feeling of pride and angry hurt.

Suggestions for stepparents

Parents who take on a household of their partner's children must love their partner very much! All parents know how critical children can be, and when they are watching your behaviour with your stepchildren, they will be even sharper to notice your mistakes. If they feel you are being unfair, or showing favouritism to their stepbrothers or sisters, there will be trouble.

Guilt, we saw in Chapter 2, is not often the problem that some people imagine; children do not necessarily feel to blame when their parents separate. But when it is a second marriage, they sometimes have good cause. Greg actually heard his stepfather say: 'Our marriage never had a chance with your children around—they ruined our happiness.' Greg found it hard to repress his joy when his mother left his stepfather, but at the same time he never forgot those words and felt a heavy burden of guilt for many years.

Guidelines for stepfamilies

There can be no hard and fast rules for living together. In fact, even the Stepfamily Association talk about guidelines for *survival* rather than for *living*! No one can presume to suggest definitive rules for stepparenting; it is a hard task and one for which there is no training, and for which too few seek counselling.

Remember firstly that *you* chose to marry. Your own children and your stepchildren *had no choice*. How do you think they feel? They are not all selfish—although naturally they are possessive of the parent they are now living with. Also, having lost one parent, they are afraid remarriage will mean losing the other one as well—help!

You must give the new family, and your marriage, *time to grow*. Expectations of everything 'sorting itself out' in a few weeks or months are not optimistic but naive—there are too many lives to consider.

Four stepparents (two mothers and two fathers) helped me sift through the professional therapists' books and theories, and they and many, many others generously shared their widely varied and sometimes dramatic experiences with me—which resulted in a list of suggestions for new stepparents. I then asked six children (two now young adults, two teenagers, and two in middle school) to check the list. Here is their edited version:

Guidelines for stepparents

(1) Always invite your children to the wedding.
(2) Tell your children what to expect from your new partner—warts and all.
(3) Do not move a child out of his room for a stepbrother or sister.
(4) Give a child plenty of time to be alone with his real mother or father, and allow him to love her/him without feeling guilty.
(5) Try to be friends to the children, not surrogate parents.
(6) Do not run down your ex-husband or wife—she/he is still your child's parent.

Quite a formidable list! But children are sticklers for justice, and agreed a list for them would be fair. They, and many others kind enough to talk with me, came up with the following guidelines (which they allowed the parents to edit):

Suggestions for stepchildren

(1) Try to be friends with your mum or dad's new partner.
(2) Do not forget your stepparent loves your parent, and that he/she is feeling just as anxious as you about the situation.
(3) Remember your stepbrothers and sisters are feeling as strange as you are.
(4) Try to behave in your stepparents' home as you do in other friends' houses.
(5) Do not compare your two homes too much—everyone is different, and has different tastes.

The only hope for success seems to be a sharing of such ideas, and a discussion of all the problems and challenges that present themselves. If both can ask help of the other it can work well: a parent can ask a teenage girl how to cook meals, or arrange rooms, to her dad's liking. A teenage boy can ask his stepfather for help with homework.

Happy families

We have looked at a great many of the tough problems facing stepchildren and their parents. What of the positive side? With the number of stepfamilies growing each year, there must be some attraction in the prospect of joining two families!

Melanie, now eighteen, has one of the happiest stories to tell:

> Mum divorced dad when I was twelve and my sister was ten. Dad married Suzanne, who also had two girls. We were jealous, but mum refused to let us sulk—she said, 'Why be sad when it's a much better feeling inside to be happy—surely two more sisters will be fun?' Dad was living three miles away and we could bike there when we wanted. Then mum married Phil who has three sons. They are great—and live with us a lot as their mum is a high-flying executive and away a lot. Now mum and Phil have another boy and dad and Suzanne have a baby girl—so that's nine of us altogether!

Somehow, that household, or rather both households, appear to work well. 'It's thanks to mum, she insists *we all spend as much time with our real parents as we want.* Of course we have problems, and lots of arguments, what family doesn't?'

Extra special children

Another mother, with two children of her own, and three stepchildren, was asked: 'How do you cope with all those extra children?' Suddenly inspired, she replied: 'I think of them, not as extra children, but *extra special children*, that's how.'

Immediately, three little faces lit up—she had picked the right words.

Even Annie, who nearly wrecked her mother's wedding, now says:

> My sister and I, and other friends I know, have all matured much earlier because of our experiences. We are fiercely loyal and far more aware that everyone has different ideas—we've learned to respect each other's wishes.

8
Grandparents

'If ever I get divorced, I won't dare tell my mother, I know she'll disapprove.'

There *are* still grandparents who find a family divorce very hard to face, and some who even cut themselves off from separating sons and daughters. This old-fashioned attitude is rare, but is a hard blow for divorcing couples and an added sorrow for their children. It is only adults who ever feel families should be split up—children never do.

Dick and Angie were eight and nine when their parents separated, and the only person Angie felt she could talk to was her grandmother. 'But grandma refused to speak to me on the telephone. She said my mum was behaving badly and that I'd become the same if I stayed with her.' Angie's father was too dominated by his own parents to help his children, who went away with their heartbroken mother and never saw their beloved grandma and grandpa again.

Their story is not unique, but thankfully it is one which is not repeated as often as 'happy' tales of grandparents who are of enormous help during a family crisis. One grandmother was the real saving of a young family. Her daughter was only 25 when her husband deserted her, leaving her with two preschool children and a baby on the way. Granny simply 'took over'. It is hard work and grandpa laughs when friends talk of his 'retirement', but the little family are growing up in a homely, loving atmosphere.

Today, the number of families in Britain who live within easy distance of aunts and uncles, cousins and grandparents is low. Running to grandpa for advice or to grandma for a fresh cookie are activities seldom enjoyed by our children. Yet grandparents can be invaluable—in practical and therapeutic terms.

The grandparent–grandchild relationship can be a very special one, and children who experience this are extremely lucky. During the predivorce days, when the home atmosphere is fraught with uncertainties and acrimony, grandparents often provide a stability for children—a warm lap to sit on, a warm meal after school, a cosy hug when there is not much love around their own house any more.

Sandy's granny saw that her little grandson was nervous one summer and found that her son and his wife were planning to divorce and had not told Sandy. Yet, at seven, he knew something was wrong. His granny was able to help his parents break the news gently and to see him through his shock and sorrow—not only at his parent's separation but at their shutting him out of their plans.

Of course, some grandparents tend to interfere—even compound the bitter arguments. 'If your mother tries to tell me how to look after the children once more, I'll not let her in the house!' We've all heard such outcries from young daughters-in-law, but if they become really serious a frail marriage can split up and the children can lose contact with loved grandparents.

'Grandpa says daddy is wicked, and he's glad you left him. Daddy's not really wicked, is he, mummy?' Sadly, grandparents can let their own bitter feelings overcome their sense of responsibility to the children—not realizing how much harm they are doing. Even when a parent has behaved badly, that must be explained to a child in terms of generosity and understanding.

Jane's grandmother used to be a lovely lady. 'Rather strict, but terribly kind to us children.' When Jane's parents divorced, grandmother became a different person. 'She was rude to mummy and said we were all selfish to turn daddy out of the house. I loved dad, but I know he used to hurt mummy and was only going away to be with his girlfriend. Granny made mummy cry even more.'

That grandmother was suffering from jealousy. Her own marriage had been a joyless one, but she had put up with it 'for the sake of the children' and now envied her daughter who was getting out of her distressing marriage. But for little Jane, granny's behaviour was an added trauma, and very sad.

Tom and his brothers were far luckier.

> Daddy's mummy was very kind to us when daddy disappeared. We thought she might be too upset and not want to see us, but she always comes to visit and is even paying for me and my brothers to go to school. She's a smashing gran.

Two sets of grandparents

Sometimes, when a divorce takes place, and there are two sets of grandparents, the arguments can move up to the older generation: 'My mother and my mother-in-law never spoke to each other again after my husband and I separated.'

A young mother's children were not allowed to see their paternal grandparents unless their mother stayed at home. At five and six they hated this, visits always meant tears, and instead of warm relationships being built up, they grew to associate grandparents with very unhappy times.

When grandparents are left out

But grandma and grandpa are not always the ones to cause the friction—far from it. It is more often one or other of the still hurt and embittered parents who can ruin wonderful grandparent–grandchild relationships—often for many, many years.

One grandmother used to help her daughter-in-law with the two little girls from their days as toddlers until they were seven and eight years old. She fetched them from school every day and gave them tea, helped them with homework, played with them, until their mother came home from work. Often they stayed with her at weekends. The girls adored their granny. Then their parents divorced, and the two girls were taken to live 100 miles away:

> We used to write to granny, but mummy told us not to as it would upset her. Then mummy said granny did not love us any more so we would not hear from her. We only found out years later that mummy had thrown away all the Christmas and birthday cards granny sent us. We thought she'd forgotten us.

The cruel feelings that acrimonious divorce can engender. . . .

Grandparents' rights

Before the Children Act 1989, heartbreaking stories abounded of grandparents who were denied any contact with their grandchildren. Most disputes arose either through family feuds, or through problems with a local authority (e.g. a child being removed into 'care'). Because of this, several organizations were formed to help grandparents to overcome their tragic difficulties (see Sources of Help). These played their part in bringing about the emphasis the new Act places on using the beneficial resources of the 'wider' family. Although not specifically mentioning grandparents, it acknowledges children's relationships with *all* family members.

Grandparents may now make applications to the court for residence or other orders. It may be necessary for them to get the court's permission to bring an application, but this will always be granted where there is a genuine issue to be decided. The Family Rights Group, The Grandparents' Federation, or your solicitor will be able to advise you. All involved in such cases, including social workers, are now recognizing the family's potential as a valuable resource to be considered as a wise alternative to authority 'care'. But sadly, in cases of inter-family disputes, a happy outcome for the children and their grandparents is still dependent largely upon the cooperation of the parent(s) concerned.

Emotions can override reason when you are bitterly hurt. When Bill's wife left him with his two sons of twelve and thirteen, his father-in-law came round offering help. Bill found he could not even speak to him, and told the boys never to go to see their grandfather. The older man was devastated: 'You may have divorced my daughter, and you can divorce us if you insist, but your children haven't divorced anyone, have they?' But Bill was adamant, and took the boys to live far away from any of their mother's family. It was his thirteen-year-old son who put into words the whole, tragic consequences of his father's divorce when talking to his teacher: 'Dad said mum had stopped loving him, but that they both loved us. He lied. If he loved us he'd let me see grandpa.'

A real family

Penny and Pat, twins of eleven, have a photo of themselves and their younger brother with their parents and grandparents. Their mother hates looking at it, and once asked them, 'Why do you keep all those awful photos of daddy's family?' Penny did not hesitate over her answer: 'It reminds us of our happy days when we were a real family.'

Another group of sad children, missing out on what could have been a happy, extended family, an extra source of much-needed love and affection during this bleak period in their lives.

Providing a neutral meeting place

In families where one, or both, sets of grandparents are actively able to take part in *both* households after a divorce, this can be a tremendous help to everyone. Immediately following the separation, they can often provide a 'neutral' ground where a parent can see his/her children before regular visits are arranged. This can lessen the strangeness of the new way of life for the younger children, and keep a contact going that might easily have drifted away. One or other partner may be longing to break right away and start a new life, perhaps a new marriage, and the idea of fixing up dates and times for their children to visit their ex-spouse is extremely disruptive to their plans. Some hardly make the effort. So if granny can step in, offer to take the children off for the day 'to see dad' or to stay with them so that mum can go out while dad visits, the children will benefit from this easy introduction to future arrangements. This is one time when granny will *not* be interfering, but assisting in her grandchildren's well-adjusted development.

Grandfather's role

When it is father who is the 'absent' parent—especially when the absence is prolonged or permanent—then a grandfather has an important role to play within a young household. Many men, in fact, seem to be better at grandparenting than parenting. The boys in the family will need that male influence, and the girls also will appreciate the male discipline, and learning the pleasure of being female. No one can ever take the place of a parent, but as Jo, aged only nine, whispered to his granny, 'Grandpa's the next best thing!'

Conflicting issues

> I wanted granny to come and see us but she says she'll never come to see us again because mummy has this lady friend. I miss my granny.

More conflicting issues arise when a daughter or son-in-law leaves home to set up a lesbian or homosexual relationship. Almost without exception, grandparents do try to interfere in these cases. They are then a huge source of comfort, providing a stable home where children can feel secure. But sometimes emotions get out of hand and then their efforts do more harm then good. Polly, at sixteen, was mature enough to face her mother's new life, and to comment that, 'It is granny who needs the counselling, not me.'

Keeping memories alive

After divorce, children's sense of belonging, of feeling part of a family, will have been damaged, and hearing stories about their father or mother's childhood and learning of their ancestors can restore a greal deal of self-esteem and confidence.

This is where a grandmother can help. Obviously it is asking too much of a parent to pore over old photo albums of happier days—but granny will love to show them. ('That's dad at school, you're just like him now.')

Becoming a step-grandparent

We have seen the effect a family divorce can have on grandparents, and the bitter rivalries and jealousies that can be aroused. What happens when they are *instant* grandparents to a completely strange set of step-grandchildren?

There may be rivalry with the natural grandparents, and perhaps difficulty in getting the children to accept them. Teenagers do not often bother to acknowledge the 'new' grandparents, and even younger ones are not necessarily ready to accept them. 'I don't want another granny, thank you. I've got two already'—Robert, aged seven, was very polite, but expressed his understandable feelings of being swamped by his new family. (They later became firm friends!)

Other children, like Annabel, may be feeling very 'left out' if their mother marries into a large family, with several children. She had never known her own grandparents who had died before she was born, and this new step-granny was exciting. The two were a great comfort to each other.

Here again, grandparents can help many children to sort out their complicated relationships. There may have been two divorces, and now two or more groups of stepbrothers and sisters, perhaps a few half-brothers and sisters also.

One grandmother made her family two large wall-charts of the family trees. Searching for old photos and records and names, she aroused the interest of all the children, and when a new 'joint' baby was born, he was written in on *both* charts. 'A sort of symbol of our united families,' said the mother. It helped those children to understand that the remarriage had not caused either family to lose its identity.

Standing-in for grandparents

I feel it is worth saying here that for children without grandparents—and there are many—aunts and uncles can often help to fill this gap and become equally good family historians and storytellers! Neighbours, too, make wonderful 'surrogate grandparents'—giving children a renewed interest in life and an experience they might otherwise miss out on.

9
How Can We All Help?

Wanting to help, knowing *how* to help, and being *able* to help are not always the same.

Some families obviously need a great deal of help, others may appear to be coping well. None of them, however, will cope sufficiently to help all their children come through the trauma of divorce and/or their parents' remarriages, without some scars.

Basically, the best way to start helping a child is to help his parents. One teenager worked this out for himself: 'Joining a divorced parents' group was the best thing mum ever did. It helps her to be with people who know what it's like. *And it's made it easier for us.*'

Friends and relations

Try to be around without intruding. Newly divorced families, however large, feel isolated. One mother was heard to say: 'Friends who are not divorced seem to be suspicious of my children—as if they may be a threat to their families.'

If mum is on her own with the children, find out if there are any male relations around; if dad is trying to manage alone, ensure that aunts and grannies are there when possible. There is a danger that their friends will be confined to those in other one-parent families, and both households need to be with couples, so the children can see that marital relationships can work, can survive arguments.

At the time of a break-up, people are so emotional; they have had a huge shock which has upset the structure of their lives. Parents are absorbed with themselves, and find it impossible to judge objectively what they should be doing for their children.

The Children's Society, with its wealth of experience with families, stresses that if we are really concerned about the long-term welfare of children, we must give more support to families. That means every type of family: the original family, the lone-parent family, and the stepfamily. Support, they say, is needed from schools; churches; government (with policies to ease financial burdens); courts (with simplified legal systems); and through more easily available social welfare.

Initially, support of friends and extended families can be sufficient—but it has to be reliable. 'My neighbour is never nosey, but I know she's there if we need her.' That's friendship.

Having said that, newly divorced parents do get huge support from joining one of the self-help groups around the country, notably Gingerbread. The local Citizens' Advice Bureau will have a list of them. My impression, on visits to their meetings, is of a large network of support, friends, *and* fun. 'Events are arranged for evenings or Sundays—all the times when the strangeness of being on your own is most noticeable. Sharing feelings, ideas, and often babysitting, is an enormous help.'

In the early days, a parent may not feel like getting involved in quite such a social way, so find out (perhaps through your doctor) if there is a 'divorce experience course', or similar, in your neighbourhood. Family therapists, or educational psychologists, will give talks perhaps once a fortnight, and there will be plenty of chance to discuss problems both with them and with other parents. As a friend, you could offer to take the children out while a parent attends these sessions—they can be supportive, and are a positive way of learning to cope. Many have special sessions for children, grouped according to age.

There are also 'home-start' schemes in some areas of the country, to provide advice for young families. They appreciate the difficulties of parents who may have experienced poor parenting themselves and received no training of any kind for this responsible role—daunting if faced alone.

Sometimes problems are too hard for parents to handle and impossible to resolve without professional help. Tell them it is not a question of blame or feeling guilty, or of being a bad parent, but of trying to understand and change the underlying pattern which lies behind their difficulty. Child guidance clinics, run by local health authorities, family therapy centres, and probation services and family welfare association counselling sessions are all means of exploring and dealing with such issues. You may find your friend reluctant to take such steps, even if she is getting desperate, so take her to see her doctor. He *may* suggest a psychiatrist, but do try to insist she sees a *family*-orientated clinic first of all—it is usually something the whole family needs to work through together.

If you are in your friend's home frequently, you may well be in a good position to create a rapport with one or more of the children, and they will welcome your attention. If you can build up a secure, trusting relationship a child may start to talk to you about a problem that he did not want to tell to his mother, for fear of upsetting her. Never try to be a therapist yourself, and assume a child is 'mentally disturbed' after watching his behaviour and diagnosing his messy drawings! It's not that simple. But *do* tell his mother if you suspect a prolonged or very distressing worry in a child, so that together you can discuss the best place to turn to for further help.

Parents

If the children are living with you

Looking after children on your own needs the strength of a saint; if you overdo the love they will resent you and never grow up to be independent; if you ignore them and concentrate on your work (which you may have to in order to feed them) they miss out on the assurance of care they desperately need.

Bear in mind that children in two-parent families are often 'deprived' of love. Families are not always the happy, secure places we like to believe they are. Few parents, even when happily married, are saints.

The only way to cope is to listen to others who have also been through those dark dreadful days: 'Sharing children's grief, crying together over our anxious moments, have strengthened the bonds between us. We're fine!'

One therapist said there are three things for a lone parent to remember: acknowledge a child's unhappiness; comfort him when upset; and reassure him that things *will* get better.

You can help your children so much just by being there—and keeping home life as close to its old routine as possible. It is more vital than ever to build up your child's self-esteem—double your efforts to praise his smallest successes, and admire the glimmering of a new talent. Does that sound like spoiling? Remember how you felt at his age. Were you always shoved aside by the adults in your home? Did it make you feel good about yourself? Give them time and attention and they will be far more willing to give the same to you.

It is worth listening to children's views here. Most of them list their anxieties while living with one parent in this order:

(1) Mum or dad saying nasty things about each other.
(2) Mum or dad not letting me see my other parent, or making me feel guilty when I do.
(3) Everyone being miserable all the time.

Yes, they *do* expect you to be a saint! But you will have seen from other chapters that if you can relieve them of those anxieties, you and they will develop a stronger relationship than ever before.

You have to be patient—it is this problem about separating 'emotionally' as well as legally, and you may not have achieved that yet. Get your friends to help, if possible the married as well as the single ones; your children need to know that a social life is still possible—they want to see you laugh as well as cry.

There is no harm in crying, of course. Let the children share your tears, it will do you all good. A child may be very nervous, full of fears—divorce is a traumatic event—so never laugh at him, or punish him. Rather say: 'Lots of children of your age are afraid of things like that—I was!' Let him see that it is natural, and all right to feel that way, and that his feelings will not last for ever. Any of your children's reactions, however strong or distressing, must be treated with respect and sympathy—never with criticism or disapproval.

What if you feel one child's fears or reactions are increasing?

How do you know if he needs professional help? Be watchful for signs of emotional stress, which are not always obvious. Often a very quiet child becomes lethargic, even sleeping longer than usual. Other signs to look out for are:

(1) Are his worries, and behaviour, inappropriate to his age?
(2) Is he slipping back to fears and habits of younger days, such as thumbsucking, bedwetting, clinging to you or an older sibling?
(3) Is he refusing school, afraid to let you out of his sight, sleeping badly?

If he is of school age, do compare notes with his teacher to see how much his behaviour in class coincides with that at home. If you have both noted changes over a prolonged period, do consult your doctor. Be firm. Never allow your child to be treated as a 'problem child'—he is a child *with a problem.* The child guidance clinic will help to find out how serious that problem is. The child may not want to attend, but will secretly be grateful that you are paying attention to him—he is longing to feel 'normal' again.

If you are living apart from your children

Your child's anxieties about the parent he is living with will affect you in the same way. He longs for your permission to *enjoy* where he is living, and to be able to mention your ex-partner's name without fear of comment. He does not want to be 'grilled' about his life at home or mum's or dad's friends. He wants to feel *you* also represent 'home' for him—not just a Saturday or Sunday place of entertainment.

It is one of the hardest situations to be in—and if you have little or no cooperation from your ex-spouse, then it is not likely to be the totally natural father–child relationship you are hoping for. The important thing is for you to show, as well as tell, your children that your feelings for them have not, *and will not*, change.

If your children are under three, you may find that it is easier for you to visit *them*, say hourly visits twice a week. Many fathers now arrange visits so that they can put a child to bed after taking him home, or bath him when a little older, so that you can become well known to him, and a real part of his life. Your older children may want to stay overnight, or for long weekends in your house. Then it will be easier not to treat them as guests, and to create a real second home.

You may feel that helping them is not so easy for you as it is for the parent they live with. This is true—but you can help by making their times with you calm and enjoyable, and they will appreciate times *alone* with you. A dad will be told things that mum is not, and vice versa—so be a receptive listener. Meeting your friends is important to them also—many children worry deeply over a parent living alone.

If you suspect your child is over-anxious, or showing unusual behaviour, do discuss this with his other parent—write it down if communication between you is difficult. Do not blame, or criticize, merely show your concern—that is what parenting is about.

If they cry on leaving their mum, or leaving you, remember it is because they love you both. Goodbyes will become less traumatic as time goes by—especially if you live near them, and visits can be more flexible as the family gets older.

It is important to keep to visiting times and days as often as possible—become a stable part of your children's lives, they need that so badly. Conversely, do not be hurt if they choose to visit friends instead of coming to your house sometimes—giving them their freedom is something *all* parents have to come to terms with.

One father, with five years' experience of living apart from his children, is quoted as saying:

> If you're concerned about the kids—and you should be concerned about them—spend a reasonable amount of time with them. I can't imagine seeing my kids only on holidays. I talk to them on the phone almost every day and see them often. Frequent contact is really important to stay in touch with what my children are doing and thinking.

If you are a stepparent

Both parents often mature following their divorce—it is a time when a man or woman finally 'grows up' and this augurs well for their second marriage. Children can also benefit from having four, instead of two adults to turn to and gain experience from as they develop. Having said that, yours is the most difficult situation of all in which to *help* your children.

You have to remember that their expectations are sure to be quite different from yours—where you are visualizing a new family, they are wondering how on earth they can live among all these strange people and *still* be loyal to their other parent. All families need time to grow, and you can best help your family by explaining this to them, and then by *still always being available to them*. Try to make time for you, and each of your children separately, to have your own space *together*—despite all the demands of your new family. Is that a daunting idea? It will pay dividends: it may well save having to call in outside help for your children: it may mean the difference between success and failure for your second marriage.

Grandparents

You are in a privileged position from which to help children. The ideas in Chapter 8 could give you a hint of the influence you can have within a family.

Of course, you must start, like everyone else, by helping their parents. That means *not* criticizing their divorce, or their ex, no matter what you feel about either—that can only be pointless and destructive.

Be available as babysitters, or as a port in the storm for troubled teenagers, and where possible as a 'neutral' place of contact for visiting parents. If you can both be seen not 'taking sides', not making one or other parent appear 'guilty', you will be giving your grandchildren the best help they will ever receive.

If either side of the family prevent you from enjoying this worthwhile role, they will be harming innocent children.

Teachers

Many children can best be helped by support from their known and respected teacher, 'rather than by direct referral to a psychologist' (and that advice comes from an educational psychologist!). For teachers are in an unrivalled position from which to assess a child and her problems. They have expertise and experience, and by liaising with the professional help at hand, as well as with the parents, they can often detect when and where the help is needed.

Parents still fight shy of telling schools of their divorce, 'because the teacher then expects trouble'. This is sad—the children then feel 'different' and some are even made to feel their parents have done something to be ashamed of. Teachers can help firstly by *not* allowing a child to feel any guilt.

It is up to head teachers to include education for 'living in harmony' along with their other extracurriculum subjects. Also to liaise with other helping agencies. Cruse, the organization for the widowed and their children, now offer Counselling Courses for teachers, which could be of great benefit when helping children cope with that other loss, divorce. Schools and teachers *do* help by becoming the most stable and secure feature of a child's disturbed life—but they can also be of extra help to those children whose distress no one in their home lives seems to have noticed.

Teenagers

Perhaps your parents have separated, and you are fed up—no one seems to care what you do, let alone how you feel. Get together with friends in the same situation and see how they are surviving it. Resist the temptation to sit in front of TV and mope; get up and do something active. So you are not a footballer and you hate swimming? Get out your bike or work out at a gym. Ever thought of joining the Ramblers' Association? You meet some great people there. Try to enrol for rock-climbing or orienteering. It takes a lot of effort but physical exercise does lift depression, far better than taking anything your doctor could prescribe; if nothing else it will take your mind off your own troubles as you swing on the end of that rope! And think how virtuous you'll feel afterwards.

I suppose it is asking too much to suggest joining a voluntary group to help disabled kids or old folk? It is always sobering to meet others worse off than yourself. I remember one fifteen-year-old having a hard time—*neither* of his parents wanted him living with them—imagine! But he went with his school to a hostel for blind children and found them climbing, even sailing. 'I'm still not proud of my parents,' he said, 'but I've worked off a lot of my anger. I'm determined not to let their behaviour spoil my life.'

If mum will not let you see your dad, or vice versa, see if your friends or grandparents can help. If you make the first gesture, mum will see that you are serious, and it will please dad no end. Try your Youth Club, or ask mum if her friends at Gingerbread have young people of your age. Maybe you belong to a church or sports club? Of course times alone are vital for everyone—but having a busy social life is the best tonic when your world seems upside down.

If you have any worrying medical problems like headaches, or an irritating rash, you can go to the school nurse, or your doctor. Some counties have special counselling services for teenagers (you may well spot a notice about this in your school or local library, or in the doctor's waiting-room). These are geared to help you and your family to cope with any distress following the break-up.

Never hesitate to ask your teacher—most people really do like being asked to help. He may also be able to guide you to the best professional help available in your town. Look up the civil work unit in the phone book; they will advise you of the nearest social welfare services. And don't avoid probation officers—all the men and women I met were nothing like the grim custodians of young people 'on probation' that we imagine; they are the kindest, most understanding group of people, with wide experience of divided families. You will find them under county court in the phone book. The Citizens' Advice Bureau will also provide any addresses or phone numbers you need.

Ask your local library for a book that might help with any specific problems; there are some that are worth sharing with your parents. They will welcome your interest—remember, they will be needing help too.

If you have younger brothers and sisters, what about taking them out? They will not understand as much as you do about relationships, and talking with you may be easier for them than talking to mum or dad.

Above all, bear in mind that things *do* calm down. Divorce does not need to mean goodbye for ever to one parent. Perhaps you have already started seeing your parents as two people, and loving them both in different ways? You will spend more time with each one on your own now, so you can take time getting to know each other. Divorce need not be the end of your world.

Listen to the children

Divorce can be the ending of a family, leaving bitterness and depression in its wake—ruining children's future hopes of happy parenting.

Divorce can be a starting point: parents often become *better* parents; children often become caring, responsible and mature young people.

Reactions are as varied as people and families. We would all do well to listen to our children:

Teenager: It cheers me up to know that once upon a time you and daddy loved each other.

Ten-year-old: I don't want to go and see mum. It hurts too much saying goodbye. I can't take any more hurting, dad.

Four-year-old: My home's not broken. It works.

Sources of Help

The Advisory Centre for Education (ACE)
1b Aberdeen Studios
22–24 Highbury Grove
London N5 2EA
0171–354 8318
Fax: 0171–354 9069
Advice line: 0171–354 8321 (open 2–5pm)

The Association for Separated and Divorced Catholics
c/o Cathedral House
250 Chapel Street
Salford
Information: 01706–352925

Both Parents Forever
39 Cloonmore Avenue
Orpington
Kent BR6 9LE
01689–854343
National Co-ordinator: John Bell

Child and Family Guidance Clinics
Ask your GP or local CAB for your nearest Clinic.

The Children's Legal Centre, University of Essex
Wivenhoe Park
Colchester
Essex CO4 3SQ
01206–872466 Administration
01206–873920 Advice service: Mon, Tues, Thurs, Fri: 2–5pm,
Wed: 10am–12noon. 24hr answer phone.

The Children's Society
Edward Rudolf House
Margery Street
London WC1X 0JL
0171–837 4299
The Society offers support to children and families under pressure.

Citizens' Advice Bureaux
CAB will offer advice, useful addresses and further sources of help. Your nearest branch will be listed in the local telephone directory.

Divorce Mediation and Counselling
38 Ebury Street
London SW1W 0LU
0171–730 2422

Family Rights Group (for children in care or at risk)
The Print House
18 Ashwin Street
London E8 3DL
0171–923 2628
Advice line: 0171–249 0008
Expert advice on all family matters.

The Family Mediators Association
North & Central London:
0181–954 6383 (Jacqueline Klarfeld)

South & Central London:
0181–789 9111 (Fiona Read)

All other areas:
0117–950 0140 (Lisa Parkinson)

Gingerbread
16–17 Clerkenwell Close
London EC1R 0AA
0171–336 8183/4
For lone parents and children. Contact Head Office for details of nationwide groups.

Grandparents' Federation
National Secretary: Noreen Tingle
Room 3, Moot House
The Stow
Harlow
Essex CM20 3AG
01279–444964
Predominantly, but not exclusively, for grandparents who have grandchildren 'In Care'.

Institute of Family Therapy Family Mediation Service
24–32 Stephenson Way
London NW1 2HX
0171–391 9150
Conciliation advice, as well as services for families in distress.

Marriage Care
Clitherow House
1 Blythe Mews
Blythe Road
London W14 0NW
0171–371 1241

Mediation in Divorce
13 Rosslyn Road
East Twickenham
Middlesex TW1 2AR
0181–891 6860/3107 (9.30am–1pm Mon–Fri)
Appointments by arrangement. Includes 'all issues' mediation.

Mothers Apart from their Children (MATCH)
c/o BM Problems
London WC1N 3XX
A nationwide self-help group (sae with enquiries please).

The National Children's Bureau
8 Wakely Street
London EC1V 7QE
0171–843 6000

National Council for One-Parent Families
255 Kentish Town Road
London NW5 2LX
0171–267 1361
Free information service includes help with welfare benefits, taxation and child support.

National Family Mediation
9 Tavistock Place
London WC1H 9SN
0171–383 5993
Co-ordinating body for independent out-of-court services nationwide.

The National Stepfamily Association
Chapel House
18 Hatton Place
London EC1N 8RU
0171–209 2460 9am–5pm Mon–Fri.
Telephone counselling: 0990–168388 (2–5pm, 7–10pm, weekdays only).

Network of Access and Child Contact Centres
St Andrew's with Castle Gate
United Reformed Church
Goldsmith Street
Nottingham NG1 5JT
0115–948 4557
Will supply details of local Centres, usually run on a voluntary and charitable basis.

Off Centre
25 Hackney Grove
London E8
0181–985 8566 or 0181–986 4016 (Mon, Thurs, Fri:10am–1pm and 2–6pm. Tues, Wed: 2–6pm)
For 13–25-year-olds, the Centre offers advice in complete confidence.

Parentline
Endway House
The End Way
Hadleigh
Essex SS7 2AN
01702–559900
National Helpline: 9am–6pm Mon-Fri; 1–6pm Sat.
A network of telephone helplines for parents under stress. Callers are given the telephone number and hours of their local Parentline.

Relate National Marriage Guidance
Head Office
Herbert Gray College
Little Church Street
Rugby CV21 3AP
01788–573241

Reunite—National Council for Abducted Children
P.O. Box 4
London WC1X 3DX
0171–404 8357
Fax: 0171–242 1512
Advice line: 0171–404 8356 (Mon, Fri: 11am–3pm; Wed: 1–8pm; Tues, Thurs: 2–5pm).

S.E. London Family Mediation Bureau
5 Upper Park Road
Bromley
Kent BR1 3HN
0181–460 4606

Solicitors Family Law Association (SFLA)
All enquiries to: Mrs Mary I'Anson, Permanent Secretary
P.O. Box 302
Orpington
Kent BR6 8QX
01689–850227
For information on local family solicitors please send sae.

The Tavistock Clinic
120 Belsize Lane
London NW3 5BA
0171–435 7111
NHS out-patient clinic which promotes the mental health of families. Contact the Child and Family Department or the Adolescent Department (ages 13–21). Adolescents over 16 can phone or write to the Young People's Counselling Service for an appointment.

Welfare and Probation Officers
Will be listed under COURTS in your local telephone directory. They will advise on your nearest Saturday/Contact Centre.

W.P.F. Counselling
23 Kensington Square
London W8 5HN
0171–937 6956
General counselling for individuals and groups.

Further Reading

Atkinson, Christine, *Step-parenting* Thorsons Publishing Group 1986

Belshaw, Chris, and Strutt, Michael, *Couples in Crisis* Victor Gollancz Ltd 1984

Bowlby, John, *Attachment and Loss*, Vol III The Hogarth Press Ltd 1980

Burgoyne, Jacqueline, *Breaking Even—Divorce, Your Children and You* Penguin Books Ltd 1984

Corman, Avery, *Kramer versus Kramer* Fontana Books/Collins 1977

Cox, Kathleen, and Desforges, Martin, *Children & Divorce, A Guide for Adults* available from: Kathleen Cox F.B.Ps.S., 6 Whinfell Court, Sheffield, S11 9QA

Cox, Kathleen M. and Desforges, Martin, *Divorce and the School* Methuen 1987

Curtis, Jill and Ellis, Virginia, *Where's Daddy?* Bloomsbury 1996

Davenport, Diana, *One-Parent Families* Sheldon Press 1979

De'Ath, Erica, *Step-parenting* Family Doctor Publications 1988

Duncan, T. R. & Duncan, D., *You're Divorced, But Your Children Aren't* Prentice Hall 1979

Dyer, Clare, *Fair To The Family* available from: Mediation in Divorce, 13 Rosslyn Road, East Twickenham, Middlesex TX1 2AR 1988

Hooper, Anne, *Divorce and Your Children* Allen & Unwin 1981

Jewett, Claudia, *Helping Children Cope with Separation & Loss* Batsford Academic & Educational 1984

Lawton, Anthony, *Parents and Teenagers* (based on the Central TV Series) Unwin Paperbacks 1985

Lovell, Ann, *The Story of a Family after Divorce* Victor Gollancz 1984

Maidment, Susan, *Child Custody and Divorce* Croom Helm 1984

McCredie, Gillian and Horrox, Alan, *Voices in the Dark* (based on the Thames TV Series) Unwin Paperbacks 1985

Mitchell, Ann, *Children in the Middle; Living through Divorce* Tavistock Publications 1985

Pringle, Dr Mia Kellmer, *The Needs of Children* Hutchinson 1975

Raphael, Kate, *A Step-Parent's Handbook* Sheldon Press 1986

Rowlands, Peter, *Saturday Parent* Unwin Paperbacks 1981

Taylor, Liz McNeill, *Bringing Up Children On Your Own* Fontana/Collins 1985

Vaughan, Diane, *Uncoupling* Methuen 1987

Viorst, Judith, *Necessary Losses* Simon and Schuster, New York 1986

Walczak, Yvette with Burns, Sheila, *Divorce: The Child's Point of View* Harper & Row 1984

Wallerstein, Judith & Kelly, Joan Berlin, *Surviving The Breakup: How Children and Parents Cope with Divorce* Grant McIntyre 1980

Whitfield, Richard (Editor) *Families Matter* (written in association with the National Family Trust) Marshall Pickering

Willans, Angela, *Divorce and Separation* Sheldon Press 1983

Winfield, Pamela, *Let's Call the Whole Thing Off* Colombus 1989

Wolff, Sula, *Children Under Stress* Penguin 1973

Books for Children

Braithwaite, Althea, *I Have Two Homes* Dinosaur Publishing 1980 (4–7 years)

Blume, Judy, *It's Not the End of the World* Pan Books 1979 (11 years +)

Brown, Laurie Krasny and Brown, Marc, *Dinosaurs Divorce* Collins (3–8 years and for parents) 1993

Kemp, Gene, *Juniper* Puffin Books 1986 (Teenagers)

Mayle, Peter, *Divorce Can Happen To The Nicest People* W. H. Allen 1979 (7 years + and a good read for divorcing parents)

Mitchell, Ann, *When Parents Split Up—Divorce Explained to Young People* Macdonald 1982

The Children's Legal Centre, *When Parents Separate—an Adviser's Guide* (available from The Children's Legal Centre) (Young adults and parents) 1982

HAVERING COLLEGE OF F & H E
144408